The Works of George Silver: Comprising "Paradoxes of Defence" [Printed in 1599 and Now Reprinted] and "Bref Instructions Vpo My Paradoxes of Defence" [Printed for the First Time from the Ms. in the British Museum]

George Silver

THE WORKS OF
GEORGE SILVER
A.D. 1599

George Siluer his Paradoxes of Defence

Paradoxes of defence, wherin is Proued the true groundes of fight to be in the Short auncient weapons, and that the Short Sword hath aduantage of the longe Rapyer and or longe Sword. and the weakenes and imperfection of the Rapyer fightes displeyed. together with an admonition to the noble, auncient, victorius, valiant, and moste braue nation of Englishmen to beware of false teachers of Defence. and howe they forsake there owne naturall fightes with a breife commendation of the noble Scienne or exercisinge of armes.

By George Siluer gentleman.

1599.

Title-page to the Preſentation Copy MS. of the "Paradoxes of Defence." (No. 34,192.)

(Reduced.)

THE WORKS OF
GEORGE SILVER

COMPRISING

"PARADOXES OF DEFENCE"

[*Printed in 1599 and now reprinted*]

AND

"BREF INSTRUCTIONS VPŌ MY PRADOXES OF DEFENCE"

[*Printed for the first time from the MS. in the British Museum*]

EDITED WITH AN INTRODUCTION BY

CYRIL G. R. MATTHEY

CAPTAIN, LONDON RIFLE BRIGADE; MEMBER OF THE LONDON FENCING CLUB; AND MEMBRE D'HONNEUR DU CERCLE D'ESCRIME DE BRUXELLES

WITH EIGHT COLLOTYPE REPRODUCTIONS FROM THE MS. IN THE BRITISH MUSEUM

LONDON

GEORGE BELL AND SONS, YORK STREET

COVENT GARDEN

1898

CHISWICK PRESS:—CHARLES WHITTINGHAM AND CO.
TOOKS COURT, CHANCERY LANE, LONDON.

INTRODUCTION.

IN 1599 a certain George Silver published a work entitled "Paradoxes of Defence, wherein is proved the trve grounds of Fight to be in the short auncient weapons, and that the short Sword hath aduantage of the long Sword or long Rapier. And the weakenesse and imperfection of the Rapier-fights displayed. Together with an Admonition to the noble, ancient, victorious, valiant, and most braue nation of Englishmen, to beware of false teachers of Defence, and how they forsake their owne naturall fights: with a briefe commendation of the noble science or exercising of Armes. *By George Siluer Gentleman.* London, Printed for Edvvard Blount. 1599.", dedicated "To the Right Honorable, my Singvlar Good Lord, Robert Earle of Essex and Ewe, Earle Marshall of England, Viscount Hereford, Lord Ferrers of Chartley, Bourchier and Louaine, Maister of the Queenes Maiesties horse, & of the Ordenance, Chancellor of the Vniuersitie of Cambridge, Knight of the most noble order of the Garter, and one of her Highnesse most honorable Priuy Counsell." This book is a small 4to volume of viii and 72 pages, containing three woodcuts—a work but little known to any save antiquaries and collectors; yet for all that it is a work which must have possessed considerable value at the time it was written, when duelling and brawling were matters of everyday occurrence.

It was in all probability very shortly afterwards that George Silver wrote "Bref Instructions vpõ my pradoxes of Defence for the true handlyng of all Mann^{r} of weapons together w^{t} the fower grownds & the fower gou^{r}nors wch gouernours are left out in my pradoxes w^{t}out the knowledge of wch no Man can fight saf." This, as its title indicates, bears very materially upon the earlier work; so much so, in fact, that the "Paradoxes" without the "Bref Instructions" cannot be considered a complete work in the sense that was evidently intended by the author when he wrote the later part. The "Bref Instructions," however, so far as can be ascertained, were never published; and there is only the MS. to show that this second and completing portion of the work was ever contemplated, much less undertaken by the author. The reason why this was not published will probably never be known, but it must have been a matter of considerable moment to have hindered the completion of a work to which he evidently attached the very greatest importance.

Be that as it may, the MS. of the "Bref Instructions"

in question existed, but remained unknown except to very few people up to about the year 1890, at which time it was discovered in the MS. Department of the British Museum by the late Mr. W. London. He was warned at the Museum to beware of assuming the work to be autograph, but he afterwards stated in a letter to Captain Hutton that he found "the educated but careless and corrupt spelling to be characteristic of Silver," and also that he "considered it to be the oldest English treatise on arms, with the exception of that on the two-hand sword in the Harleian MS. (3542), which dates from the fifteenth century." The "Bref Instructions" consist of thirty-four closely-written pages in very good preservation there being but few places, and those of comparative insignificance, where the handwriting is too faded to be legible; in such cases the context, however, clearly conveys the meaning. It is interesting to note that the MS.* of the "Paradoxes" is also in the Library of the British Museum, having been purchased in 1892 at the sale of the MSS. of Edwin H. Laurence, Lot 603, at a cost of £11.

From the time that the MS. of "Bref Instructions" first became known to Mr. London he appears to have studied it with considerable care, and, although not himself a fencer, he became at once so convinced of the prac-

* MS. 47 pages. No. 34,192. "With 'Epistle Dedecatorie' (ff. 4-6) to Robert [Devereux, 2nd] Earl of Essex. Probably the actual presentation copy, &c." Vide Thimm's "Bibliography of Fencing and Duelling."

tical value to swordsmen of its contents that he made a complete transcript of it—by no means a light undertaking when the caligraphy and spelling are taken into account.

Knowing Captain Alfred Hutton by reputation as one of the most universally recognized authorities on all matters respecting the sword and its employment, it occurred to Mr. London after completing the transcript that Captain Hutton was of all others the one best qualified by his practical knowledge and experience to pronounce definitely upon the merits of the MS. He accordingly obtained an introduction, and, after some correspondence, left the transcript for perusal. This occurred in 1894. In due course it was returned, and then only Captain Hutton learned of the rather sudden death of the lender, who it appeared had some short time previously expressed a wish that the transcript might be allowed to remain in Captain Hutton's magnificent collection of fencing and duelling literature.

Thus it was, in 1895, that the "Bref Instructions," by far the more valuable part of George Silver's work, first came under my notice.

Realizing the value of this unpublished work Captain Hutton eventually extracted from Mr. London's transcript of it the material upon which he based a most interesting article in "The Indian Fencing Review" of January, 1897, on "Sword Fighting and Sword Play," constituting in itself a highly practical little work, and likely to prove of much assistance to the infantry officer desirous of rendering himself as "handy" as possible with his sword at close quarters. More recently still, namely, on September 25, 1897, Captain Hutton gave practical illustration of the "grips" mentioned by him in that article at an exhibition of swordsmanship at the Whitton Park Club, and this display following upon the publication of his paper immediately recalled to my mind the original MS. at the British Museum. I took an early opportunity of consulting this in order to make a closer acquaintance with Silver's later and more important work, which is probably the earliest (in English, at any rate) to teach what is now considered to be the most telling and classic style of fence, viz., "Parry and Riposte."

Much impressed by what I saw and afterwards read, it struck me that a work so peculiarly English, containing so much matter of value to all swordsmen, and to infantry officers in particular, ought not to remain buried, but should rather be published for the use of those who care to read and learn. I therefore determined to complete the work so nearly finished by George Silver, by publishing his MS. of "Bref Instructions." Captain Hutton and Captain Thimm, whom I consulted on this idea, gave me every encouragement, the former most kindly placing at my disposal the transcript made by Mr. London for comparison when my own transcript was completed.

After reading the "Bref Instructions" carefully through in conjunction with the "Paradoxes," I determined to make the work really complete, as George Silver had evidently intended it to be, by reprinting the "Paradoxes" as nearly as possible in their original form, with the "Bref Instructions" following *literatim et verbatim* in accordance with the MS., and in the same style as the "Paradoxes."

These latter alone contain much to interest the swordsman and the antiquary, but it is not so much to this portion of the work as to the "Bref Instructions" that I desire to direct attention, owing to the remarkably clear and concise manner in which much excellent and serviceable advice upon the handling of the sword is given. Taking into consideration the fact that the weapon recommended by Silver as the most serviceable nearly 300 years ago, though slightly longer and double-edged, was for all practical purposes similar, as regards the blade, to the regulation weapon of to-day, much, if not all, that he has written upon the handling of it in his time may well prove of immense service to those whose lives are at times dependent upon the more or less ready use of their swords.

The fact that so little distinction is now made between the swordsmanship of the duellist and that of the soldier must be incomprehensible to the majority of fencers who have given any consideration to the matter as thus defined. Fencing as now taught throughout Europe is made, and always has been, entirely subservient to the requirements of the duel, with all its attendant etiquette. This distinction is demonstrated by almost any work (whether of ancient or of modern date) upon the art of sword-fencing, and it is moreover a rule to which there are few exceptions. That this distinction should exist among continental nations cannot be altogether a matter of surprise to us, seeing that the possibility, and even, in certain countries, the probability of a duel is common to both civil and military society alike, but that this method should be adopted in this country, where duelling is altogether a thing of the past, it is not quite so easy to understand.

As a means simply of promoting health, and as a recreation, fencing of the classic schools, whether French or Italian, cannot be too highly commended, and with simply such objects as these in view all the stringent etiquette of the duel and the extreme niceties of the art of fence should be strongly insisted upon in the fencing-room. It is generally admitted that the true basis of all scientific swordsmanship is foil-play—meaning thereby that a man who is fairly expert with the foil will very soon render himself equally so with the sabre; although I do not suggest that a man cannot become a good sabre fencer without the groundwork of foil-fencing—I merely say that he is invariably the better for it.

Now in all probability the only Englishmen to whom swordsmanship can ever be a matter of real necessity are officers in Her Majesty's Navy and Army, of whom it is perhaps the infantry officer rather than any other that should be considered on this account, and who in particular should be clearly instructed in the vast distinction that exists between the sabre duel and the sabre fight, shorn of all formality and rules, as he would find it on service, whether against a savage or a civilized enemy. The method of instruction as at present authorized for his use is so closely allied to the duelling system as to be practically indistinguishable from it, and to such an extent is this true that the authority responsible for its invention and adoption has seen fit not only to neglect all instruction respecting either the attack or defence of the lower limbs, but has actually gone so far as absolutely to prohibit the attack or defence of any part of the body below the hip. From this, and from many other instances of a more or less similar nature, it is evident beyond dispute that the system and etiquette of the duel have been rigidly adhered to throughout, and this too in a text-book presumably compiled to teach *free sabre fighting*, such as would be encountered on active service. Clearly, in the place of this, a simple system should have been drawn up to teach an officer how to defend himself thoroughly, and how to attack an adversary, without puzzling him with a number of complicated parries and movements, which, even if practicable with a feather-weight duelling sabre, and in the fencing-room, become utterly impossible with the regulation sword, and in a fight of the "rough and tumble" order. Given the present infantry regulation sword of sufficient weight and strength to render it a really serviceable weapon, it would be impossible for any man to put into practice the principles which he is now supposed to be taught. Why not, therefore, having decided upon the pattern of the regulation sword, have drawn up, or have caused to be drawn up, by one or more of our well-known swordsmen, competent from experience to judge what is really requisite for the purpose, a simple common-sense method of *sword-fighting* suitable for service requirements. This could easily be taught, and devoid of a great deal of that preliminary fencing-room drudgery that so frequently proves to be the real bar to further interest and improvement except in the case of the enthusiast—a system, in fact, of such a description that the advanced "science" of the sword is as far as possible eliminated from it, in order to make way for the simple development of individual coolness and quickness by such means as can without difficulty be practised by officers among themselves at any time.

That such a system can be drawn up, and that there are those who are thoroughly qualified to do it well, there is no doubt—the main point to be borne in mind being from the outset to dismiss all that to any unnecessary extent savours of the duelling school, and then to teach the smallest number and the simplest of parries that will protect a man *from head to foot*, and the *correct and quickest way* of delivering a cut or thrust, coupled with careful instruction in the judicious use of the left hand in defence, which is now and has long been totally ignored. So soon as an officer instructed upon such simple lines as these finds that he can always stop deliberate attacks delivered without feints (as they might usually be expected), and can make his ripostes with tolerable hope of success, he will at once begin to acquire confidence in himself and in his sword at close quarters, and before long it is not unreasonable to believe that our officers generally would learn properly to understand, and to form a more correct estimate of the value of the weapons they wear as a fighting arm, than with certain almost rare exceptions is at present the case.

The whole matter practically then amounts to this: In order to make a man a fencer it requires an expenditure of much time, patience, and labour on the part of instructor and pupil alike. Why therefore endeavour to achieve so much which at the best can only be done in comparatively few cases, whereas far more practical results can be attained, and that in a much larger number of cases, with infinitely less trouble to all concerned? Surely, if an officer after practical experience found that he could hold his own and render a good account of himself in a hand-to-hand encounter on such lines as already suggested, is it not also reasonable to suppose that this of itself would prove sufficient incentive to him to look into the real "science" of the art of his own accord, and thus eventually to assist, though in a way unintentionally, in the re-establishment of the art of fence in this country upon an even better, and certainly upon a more justifiable basis than that upon which it exists in other countries?

To the infantry officer, then, whether he be a fencer or

not, and perhaps more especially in the latter case, I earnestly recommend a perusal and careful study of the "Bref Instructions;" for I am convinced that a great deal of what he reads therein can be put into practice in sword encounters with highly successful results, especially when they take place against men of savage or barbarian races that Her Majesty's troops are now so frequently sent to face in various quarters of the globe. To him I particularly commend the "Gryps" (cap. 6), and the ripostes that can be made from them—powerful parries, with strong, rapid, and, in the majority of cases, most unlooked-for ripostes, calculated to thoroughly surprise an adversary under almost any circumstances.

As an example: A rushing opponent delivers a sweeping downward blow at the left side of the head or neck. This is met with a high prime parry, and nothing being less likely than a feint under such circumstances, the blow can be met deliberately, or even with a forward movement of the foot, and the assailant's sword-wrist gripped firmly with the left hand under the right as his cut is checked, and almost simultaneously with the formation of the parry. The sword-point is then inclined to the rear over the left shoulder, and the pommel dashed into his face with terrific force, the way being further cleared for it by pressure downwards with the left hand upon the adversary's sword-arm. There are, of course, variations of this, and a man fairly practised in this class of close fighting would be able easily to combine all these movements almost into a single action; and there is, moreover, a great point in favour of this, inasmuch as it is hardly possible for any defence to be brought against a riposte of this kind in time to prove successful. The more furious and determined the onslaught the simpler and more effective the parry and riposte really become. Silver gives the "gryps" or seizures for use to meet various attacks with ripostes of this description (in many cases with the alternative of using the point), which can most effectively be made from them, and these it is which appear of such practical value as to warrant the publication of them after so many years of oblivion.

It is true that they had gone out of vogue before his time, as is shown by his statement in the "Paradoxes," that "there are now in these dayes no gripes, closes, wrestlings, striking with the hilts, daggers, or bucklers, vsed in Fence-schools," but which at the same time proves them to have been previously recognized, taught, and used, and to have simply been lost sight of as times and weapons changed.

It is sufficiently remarkable that from the very commencement Silver lays great stress upon defence; every argument he makes use of points to the absolute necessity of this in the first instance, and it is only when in safety that he advises counter-attack or riposte.

The soundness of his views in this is amply justified by the fact that the most classic fence of the present day is admitted by schools of fence of all nations to consist of the correctly-formed parry followed by an instantaneous riposte. He draws particular attention to the fact that for years previous to his time all had been sacrificed to attack, and that defence had been almost if not entirely neglected for the sake of attack by those who made it their business to teach the use of the sword—a fact which he justly condemns. This remains the point of primary importance throughout Silver's work, and forms the very essence of his teaching.

Much that we can read in the "Paradoxes" appears to have been, and doubtless was, written in a feeling of intense irritation against and jealousy of Saviolo (the writer on the rapier)* and his school, but the manner in which he treats his own method of defence and attack in his "Bref Instructions," as opposed to that of the Italian school of his day, clearly proves that he had thoroughly thought out the system which he advocated, and that he had reduced it to a science practically of his own creation, which is remarkable at any rate for much common sense, and in some respects, perhaps, for teaching of a unique kind. His "Bref Instructions" can be still used with great effect, almost without modification, to suit our modern sword, and it is on this account that I have brought them forward, suppressing or adding no-

* "Vincentio Saviolo. His Practise, in two bookes: the first treating of the Use of the Rapier and Dagger, the second of Honour and Honourable Quarrels. 4to, 1595. London: Printed by John Wolfe."

thing, in order to show how wide a scope they still possess for providing a powerful method of defence against all weapons, and some simple though telling ripostes for use in hand-to-hand fighting. Silver, too, fully realized the fact that the hilt or pommel of the sword (or the butt of any arm) constituted an effectively offensive portion of the weapon if properly handled. A few modern authors, who have written upon bayonet fighting, have taught the use of the rifle-butt, but Silver was, so far as I have been able to ascertain, the first writer to attach any importance to the offensive possibilities of the sword-hilt. That in it he indicates a weapon of great power, when used as an auxiliary to the point and edge at close quarters, there can be no doubt, for whereas many a man can do much damage to his opponent after being run through the body, especially if able for the moment to retain the blade in himself (and thus render his enemy momentarily powerless), few if any would be able to stand up against a back-handed blow in the face with the pommel of a regulation sword.

I suggest that sword *fighting* is not taught, and that it ought to be. Fencing should be encouraged to the utmost, but fighting should be regarded, as it was by Silver, as a distinct subject, and of much greater importance in the majority of cases.

My advice to every infantry officer is to study these grips closely, and to thoroughly master the simplicities of sword fighting, and on no account to try to persuade himself that an intricate and possibly faulty duelling school will keep his skin whole in hand-to-hand fighting, unless he be already an expert fencer.

CYRIL G. R. MATTHEY.

TO THE RIGHT HONORABLE, MY SINGVLAR GOOD LORD, ROBERT EARLE OF Eſſex and Ewe, Earle Marſhall of England, Viſcount Hereford, Lord Ferrers of Chartley, Bourchier *and Louaine, Maiſter of the Queenes Maieſties horſe*, & of the Ordenance, Chancellor of the Vniuerſitie of Cambridge, *Knight of the moſt noble order of the Garter, and one of her Highneſſe moſt honorable Priuy Counſell.*

FENCING (Right honorable) in this new fangled age, is like our faſhions, euerie daye a change, reſembling the Camelion, who altereth himſelfe into all colours ſaue white: ſo Fencing changeth into all wards ſaue the right. That it is ſo, experience teacheth vs: why it is ſo, I doubt not but your wiſedome doth conceiue. There is nothing permanent that is not true, what can be true that is vncertaine? how can that be certaine, that ſtands vpon vncertain grounds? The mind of man a greedie hunter after truth, finding the ſeeming truth but chaunging, not alwayes one, but alwayes diuerſe, forſakes the ſuppoſed, to find out the aſſured certaintie: and ſearching euery where ſaue where it ſhould, meetes with all ſaue what it would. VVho ſeekes & finds not, ſeekes in vaine; who ſeekes in vaine, muſt if he wil find ſeeke againe: and ſeeke he may againe and againe, yet all in vaine. VVho ſeekes not what he would, as he ſhould, and where he ſhould, as in all other things (Right honourable) ſo in Fencing: the mind deſirous of truth, hunts after it, and hating falſhood, flies from it, and therfore hauing miſſed it once, it aſſayes the ſecond time: if then he thriues not, he tries another way: whẽ that hath failed he aduentures on the third: & if all theſe faile him, yet he neuer faileth to chaunge his weapon, his fight, his ward, if by any meanes he may compaſſe what he moſt affects: for becauſe men deſire to find out a true defence for themſelues in their fight, therefore they ſeeke it diligently, nature hauing taught vs to defend our ſelues, and Art teaching how: and becauſe we miſſe it in one way we chaunge to another. But though

though we often chop and change, turne and returne, from ward to ward, from fight to fight, in this vnconſtant ſearch, yet wee neuer reſt in anie, and that becauſe we neuer find the truth: and therefore we neuer find it, becauſe we neuer ſeeke it in that weapon where it may be found. For, to ſeeke for a true defence in an vntrue weapon, is to angle on the earth for fiſh, and to hunt in the ſea for Hares: truth is ancient though it ſeeme an vpſtart: our forefathers were wiſe, though our age account them fooliſh, valiant though we repute them cowardes: they found out the true defence for their bodies in ſhort weapons by their wiſdome, they defended them ſelues and ſubdued their enemies, with thoſe weapons with their valour. And (Right honorable) if we will haue this true Defence, we muſt ſeeke it where it is, in ſhort Swords, ſhort Staues the halfe Pike, Partiſans, Gleues, or ſuch like weapons of perfect lẽgths, not in long Swords, long Rapiers, nor frog pricking Poiniards: for if there be no certain grounds for Defence, why do they teach it? if there be, why haue they not found it? Not becauſe it is not: to ſay ſo, were to gaineſay the truth: but becauſe it is not cer-

English maiſters of defence, are profitable members in the common wealth, if they teach with ancient Engliſh weapons of true Defence, weight and conuenient length, within the compaſſe of the ſtatures and ſtrength of men to command, becauſe it maketh them ſafe, bold, valiant, hardie, ſtrong and healthfull, and victorious in the warres, ſeruice of their Prince, defence of their friendes and countrey.

But the Rapier in reaſon not to be taught, nor ſuffred to be taught, becauſe it maketh men fearefull and vnſafe in ſingle combat, and weak, & vnſeruiceable in the warres.

taine in thoſe weapons which they teach. To proue this, I haue ſet forth theſe my Paradoxes, different I confeſſe from the maine current of our outlandiſh teachers, but agreeing I am well aſſured to the truth, and tending as I hope to the honor of our Engliſh nation. The reaſon which moued me to aduenture ſo great a taske, is the deſire I haue to bring the truth to light, which hath long time lyen hidden in the caue of contempt, while we like degenerate ſonnes, haue forſaken our foreſathers vertues with their weapons, and haue luſted like men ſicke of a ſtrange ague, after the ſtrange vices and deuiſes of Italian, French and Spaniſh Fencers, litle remembring, that theſe Apiſh toyes could not free Rome from Brennius ſacke, nor Fraunce from King Henrie the fift his conqueſt. To this deſire to find out truth the daughter of time, begotten of Bellona, I was alſo moued, that by it I might remoue the great loſſe of our Engliſh gallants, which we daily ſuffer by theſe imperfect fights, wherein none vndertake the combat, be his cauſe neuer ſo good, his cũning neuer ſo much, his ſtrength and agilitie neuer ſo great, but his vertue was tied to fortune: happie man, happie

doale,

doale , kill or be killed is the dreadfull iſſue of this diuelliſh imperfect fight. If that man were now aliue, which beat the Maiſter for the ſcholers fault , becauſe he had no better inſtructed him , theſe Italian Fencers could not eſcape his cenſure , who teach vs Offence , not Defence, and to fight , as Diogenes ſcholers were taught to daunce, to bring their liues to an end by Art. VVas Aiax a coward becauſe he fought with a ſeuen foulded Buckler, or are we mad to go naked into the field to trie our fortunes, not our vertues? VVas Achilles a run-away , who ware that well tempered armour , or are we deſperat, who care for nothing but to fight, and learn like the Pigmeys, to fight with bodkins, or weapons of like defence? Is it valour for a man to go naked againſt his enemie? why then did the Lacedemonians puniſh him as deſperate, whom they rewarded for his vallour with a Lawrell crowne? But that which is moſt ſhamefull, they teach mẽ to butcher one another here at home in peace, wherewith they cannot hurt their enemies abrode in warre. For, your Honour well knowes, that when the battels are ioyned , and come to the charge, there is no roome for them

To this it will be obiected, that in the warres we vſe few Rapiers or none at all, but ſhort Swords. To that I anſwere: Theſe are inſufficient alſo, for that they haue no

hilts, whereby they are insufficient in their defence, and especially for the hād, which being stroken although with a verie smal blow, most commonly is the losse of a mā, because the force of his hand being taken from him, he is neither able to defend his life, nor greatly to offend his enemy: and againe, since the Rapier-fight hath bene taught, for lacke of practise they haue lost the vse of the blow.

to drawe their Bird-spits, and when they haue them, what can they doe with them? can they pierce his Corslet with the point? can they vnlace his Helmet, vnbuckle his Armour, hew asunder their Pikes with a *Stocata*, a *reuersa*, a *Dritta*, a *Stramason*, or other such like tēpestuous termes? no, these toyes are fit for children, not for men, for stragling boyes of the Campe, to murder poultrie, not for men of Honour to trie the battell with their foes. Thus I haue (right Honorable) for the trial of the truth, betweene the short Sword and the long Rapier, for the sauing of the liues of our English gallants, who are sent to certaine death by their vncertaine fights, & for abandoning of that mischieuous and imperfect weapon, which serues to kill our friēds in peace, but cānot much hurt our foes in warre, haue I at this time giuen forth these Paradoxes to the view of the world. And because I knowe such straunge opinions had need of stout defence, I humbly craue your Honorable protection, as one in whom the true nobility of our victorious Auncestors hath taken vp his residence. It will sute to the rest of your Honours most noble cōplements, to maintaine the defence of their weapons whoſe vertues you poſſeſſe. It agrees with your Honourable diſpoſition, to receiue with fauour what is preſented with loue. It ſorts with your Lordſhips high authority, to weigh with reaſon, what is fit for marſhall men. It is an vſuall point of your Honor, which winnes your Lordſhip loue in your countrey, to defend the truth in whomſoeuer: and it addeth a ſupply to that vvhich your Lordſhip haue of late begun to your vnſpeakeable honor and our ineſtimable benefite, to reduce the vvearing of ſwordes vvith hilts ouer the hands, to the Romane diſcipline, no longer then they might draw them vnder their armes, or ouer their ſhoulders. In all or any of theſe reſpects, I reſt aſſured that your Lordſhip vvill vouchſafe to receiue vvith fauor and maintaine vvith honour theſe Paradoxes of mine, vvhich if they be ſhrouded vnder ſo ſafe a ſhield, I vvill not doubt but to maintaine vvith reaſon amongſt the vviſe, and proue it by practiſe vpon the ignorant, that there is no certaine defence in the Rapier, and that there is great aduantage in the ſhort Sword againſt the long Rapier, or all maner of Rapiers in generall, of vvhat length ſoeuer. And that the ſhort Staffe

Why ſhould we leaue the hand naked, ſince therby our limmes & liues are defended, our enemies diſcomforted, wounded, and executed? I ſee no reaſon but that the hand ſhould be as well armed and prouided for, as anie other part of the bodie.

hath the vauntage againſt the long Staffe of twelue, foureteene, ſixteene or eighteene foote long, or of what length ſoeuer. And againſt two men vvith their Swordes and Daggers, or two Rapiers, Poiniards & Gantlets, or each of them a caſe of Rapiers : vvhich vvhether I can performe or not, I ſubmit for triall to your Honors martiall cenſure , being at all times readie to make it good, in vvhat maner, and againſt vvhat man ſoeuer it ſhall ſtand vvith your Lordſhips good liking to appoint. And ſo I humbly commend this booke to your Lordſhips vviſedome to peruſe, and your Honour to the Higheſt to protect in all health and happineſſe novve and euer.

Your Honors in all dutie,

George Siluer.

To the most renowmed Nobillitie of England, to all noble and honnorable gentlemen and to all other of the Auncient victorious, valiant, And most brave nation of Englishmen.

George Silver havinge the true beinge in the perfect knowledge of all manner of weapons and beinge experienced in all manner of fightes thereby perceyvinge the great abuse by the Italian teachers of Offence don unto them, the great errors, inconveniences, and false resolutions they have brought them into: hath enforced me even of pittie of theire most lamentable murders and slaughters, and as in dutie therto it is my bounden dutie in the all love and humillitie to admonishe them to take heede, how they submitt them selves into the handes of Italian teachers of defence or strangers whatsoever and to beware how they forsake or suspect theire owne naturall fight, that they may by castinge of these Italionated, weake, and ffantasticall, and most divellishe and imperfect fightes, and by exercisinge of theire owne Auncient weapons, againe be restored or atcheived unto theire most naturall, and most manlie and victorious fight, the dint or force

wherof

Facsimile of page 8 of the "Paradoxes of Defence."

(Reduced.)

AN ADMONITION
TO THE NOBLE, ANCIENT, VICTORIOVS, VALIANT, AND MOST BRAVE NATION OF ENGLISHMEN.

GEorge *Siluer* hauing the perfect 1
knowledge of all maner of weapōs, and being experiēced in all maner of fights, thereby perceiuing the great abuſes by the *Italian* Teachers of Offence done vnto them, the great errors, inconueniences, & falſe reſolutions they haue brought them into, haue inforced me, euen of pitie of their moſt lamentable wounds and ſlaughters, & as I verily thinke it my bounden dutie, with all loue and humilitie to admoniſh them to take heed, how they ſubmit themſelues into the hands of *Italian* teachers of Defence, or ſtraungers whatſoeuer; and to beware how they forſake or ſuſpect their owne naturall fight, that they may by caſting off of theſe Italianated, weake, fantaſticall, and moſt diuelliſh and imperfect fights, and by exerciſing of their owne ancient weapons, be reſtored, or atchieue vnto their natural, and moſt manly and victorious fight againe, the dint and force whereof manie

braue nations haue both felt and feared. Our ploughmen haue mightily preuailed againſt them, as alſo againſt Maiſters of Defence both in Schooles and countries, that haue taken vpon thē to ſtand vpon Schooletrickes and iugling gambolds: whereby it grew to a common ſpeech among the countrie-men, Bring me to a Fencer, I will bring him out of his fence trickes with good downe right blowes, I will make him forget his fence trickes I will warrant him. I ſpeake not againſt Maiſters of Defence indeed, they are to be honoured, nor againſt the Science, it is noble, and in mine opiniō to be preferred next to Diuinitie; for as Diuinitie preſerueth the ſoule from hell and the diuell, ſo doth this noble Science defend the bodie from wounds & ſlaughter. And moreouer, the exerciſing of weapons putteth away aches, griefes, and diſeaſes, it increaſeth ſtrength, and ſharpneth the wits, it giueth a perfect iudgement, it expelleth melancholy, cholericke and euill conceits, it keepeth a man in breath, perfect health, and long life. It is vnto him that hath the perfection thereof, a moſt friendly and comfortable companion when he is alone, hauing but only his weapon about him, it putteth him out of all feare, & in the warres and places of moſt danger it maketh him bold, hardie, and valiant.

And for as much as this noble and moſt mightie nation of Engliſhmen, of their good natures, are alwayes moſt louing, verie credulous, & ready to cheriſh & protect ſtrāgers: yet that through their good natures they neuer more by ſtrangers or falſe teachers may be deceiued, once againe I am moſt humbly to admoniſh thē, or ſuch as ſhal find in themſelues a diſpoſition or deſire to learne their weapons of them, that from henceforth as

ſtran-

ſtrangers ſhall take vpon them to come hither to teach this noble & moſt valiant, & victorious nation to fight, that firſt, before they learne of them, they cauſe a ſufficient triall of them to be made, whether the excellencie of their skill be ſuch as they profeſſe or no, the triall to be very requiſite & reaſonable, euen ſuch as I my ſelfe would be contented withall, if I ſhould take vpon me to go in their countrie to teach their nation to fight. And this is the triall: they ſhall play with ſuch weapōs as they profeſſe to teach withall, three bouts apeece with three of the beſt Engliſh Maiſters of Defence, & three bouts apeece with three vnskilful valiant men, and three bouts apeece with three reſolute men half drunke. Then if they can defend thēſelues againſt theſe maiſters of Defence, and hurt, and go free from the reſt, then are they to be honored, cheriſhed, and allowed for perfect good teachers, what countrey men ſoeuer they be: but if of anie of theſe they take foile, then are they imperfect in their profeſſion, their fight is falſe, & they are falſe teachers, deceiuers and murtherers, and to be puniſhed accordingly, yet no worſe puniſhment vnto them I wiſh, then ſuch as in their triall they ſhall find.

A great fauor to giue them choice of their weapons, becauſe profeſſors of armes ought to be skilfull with all maner of weapōs.

There are foure eſpeciall markes to know the Italian fight is imperfect. & that the Italian teachers and ſetters forth of books of Defence, neuer had the perfection of the true fight.

The firſt marke is, they ſeldome fight in their owne country vnarmed, commonly in this ſort, a paire of Gantlettes vpon their hands, and a good ſhirt of maile vpon their bodies. 2

Yet they perſwade vs that the croſſe of the Rapier without hilt or gantlet is ſufficient.

The ſecōd marke is, that neither the Italians, nor any

of their beſt ſcholers do neuer fight, but they are moſt cōmonly ſore hurt, or one or both of them ſlaine.

The third marke is, they neuer teach their ſcholers, nor ſet downe in their bookes anie perfect lengthes of their weapons, without the which no man can by nature or Art againſt the perfect lẽgth fight ſafe, for being too ſhort, their times are too long, and ſpaces too wide for their defence, and being too long, they wilbe vpon euerie croſſe that ſhall happen to be made, whether it be done by skil or chance, in great danger of death; becauſe the Rapier being too long, the croſſe cannot be vndone in due time, but may be done by going backe with the feete; but that time is alwaies too long to anſwere the time of the hand, therfore euery man ought to haue a weapon according to his owne ſtature: the tall man muſt haue his weapon longer then the man of meane ſtature, or elſe he hath wrong in his defence, & the man of meane ſtature muſt haue his weapon longer then the man of ſmal ſtature, or else he hath wrong in his defence; & the man of ſmal ſtature muſt beware that he feed not himſelf with this vaine cõceipt, that he wil haue his weapon long, to reach as farre as the tall man, for therin he ſhal haue great diſaduantage, both in making of a ſtrong croſſe, and alſo in vncroſſing againe, and in keeping his point from croſſing, and when a croſſe is made vpon him, to defend himſelf, or indanger his enemie, or to redeeme his loſt times. Againe Rapiers longer, then is conuenient to accord with the true ſtatures of men, are alwaies too long or too heauie to keepe their bodies in due time from the croſſe of the light ſhort ſword of perfect length, the which being made by the skilfull out of any of the foure true times, vpon any of the foure chiefe

Acti-

Actions, by reason of the vncertaintie & great swiftnesse in any of these times, they are in great danger of a blow, or of a thrust in the hand, arme, head, body, or face, & in euerie true crosse in the vncrossing, in great danger of a blow vpon the head, or a full thrust in the bodie or face: and being taken in that time & place, the first mouer in vncrossing speedeth the Rapier man of imperfect lẽgth, whether it be too long, too short or too heauie, and goeth free himselfe by the direction of his gouernours.

The fourth marke is, the crosses of their Rapiers for true defence of their hands are imperfect, for the true cariage of the guardant fight, without the which all fights are imperfect.

Of sixe chiefe causes, that many valiant men thinking themselues by their practises to be skilfull in their weapons, are yet manie times in their fight sore hurt, and manie times slaine by men of small skill, or none at all.

THe first and chiefest cause is, the lacke of the foure Gouernours, without the which it is impossible to fight safe, although a man should practise most painfully and most diligently all the daies of his life. 3

The second cause is, the lacke of knowledge in the due obseruance of the foure Actions, the which we cal bent, spent, lying spent, and drawing backe: these Actions euerie man fighteth vpon, whether they be skilfull or vnskilfull, he that obserueth them is safe, he that obserueth thẽ not, is in cõtinuall danger of euerie thrust that shalbe strongly made against him.

The third cause is, they are vnpractised in the foure true times, neither do they know the true times frō the false: therefore the true choise of their times are most commonly taken by chance, and seldome otherwise.

The fourth cause is, they are vnacquainted out of what fight, or in what maner they are to answer the variable fight: and therefore because the variable fight is the most easiest fight of all other, most cōmonly do answer the variable fight with the variable fight, which ought neuer to be but in the first distance, or with the short Sword against the long, because if both or one of them shall happen to prese, and that in due time of neither sidefight be changed, the distance, by reason of narrownesse of space, is broken, the place is won and lost of both sides, then he that thrusteth first, speedeth: if both happen to thrust together, they are both in dāger. These things sometimes by true times, by change of fights, by chance are auoided.

The fift cause is, their weapons are most commonly too long to vncrosse without going backe with the feet.

The sixt cause is, their weapons are most commonly too heauie both to defend and offend in due time, & by these two last causes many valiāt mē haue lost their liues.

What is the cause that wise men in learning or practising their weapons, are deceiued with Italian Fencers.

No fight perfect that is not done in force & true time.

THere are foure causes: the first, their schoolmaisters are imperfect: the second is, that whatsoeuer they teach, is both true & false; true in their demōstrations, according with their force & time in gētle play, & in their

actions

actions according with true force & time in rough play or fight, falſe: for exāple, there is as much difference betwixt theſe two kind of fights, as there is betwixt the true picture of Sir *Beuis* of *Southampton*, & Sir *Beuis* himſelf, if he were liuing. The third, none cā iudge of the Craft but the Crafts-man; the vnskilfull, be he neuer ſo wiſe, can not truly iudge of his teacher, or skill, the which he learneth, being vnskilful himſelfe. Laſtly, & to confirme for truth all that ſhal be amiſſe, not only in this excellēt Science of Defence, but in all other excellent ſecrets, moſt commonly the lye beareth as good a ſhew of truth, as truth it ſelfe.

Of the falſe reſolutions and vaine opinions of Rapier-men, and of the danger of death thereby enſuing.

IT is a great queſtion, & eſpecially amōgſt 4
the Rapier-men, who hath the vantage of the thruſter, or of the warder. Some hold ſtrongly, that the warder hath the vantage: others ſay, it is moſt certain that the thruſter hath the vantage. Now when two do happē to fight, being both of one mind, that the thruſter hath the vantage, they make all ſhift they can, who ſhall giue the firſt thruſt: as for example, two Captaines at *Southampton* euen as they were going to take ſhipping vpon the key, fel at ſtrife, drew their Rapiers, and preſently, being deſperate, hardie or reſolute, as they call it, with all force and ouer great ſpeed, ran with their rapiers one at the other, & were both ſlaine. Now when two of the contrary opinion ſhall meet and fight, you ſhall ſee verie peaceable warres betweene them: for they verily thinke that he

that firſt thruſteth is in great danger of his life, therefore with all ſpeede do put themſelues in ward, or Stocata, the ſureſt gard of all other, as *Vincentio* ſaith, and therevpon they ſtand ſure, ſaying the one to the other, thruſt and thou dare; and ſaith the other, thruſt and thou dare, or ſtrike or thruſt and thou dare, ſaith the other: then ſaith the other, ſtrike or thruſt and thou dare for thy life. Theſe two cunning gentlemen ſtanding long time together, vpon this worthie ward, they both depart in peace, according to the old prouerbe: It is good ſleeping in a whole skinne. Againe if two ſhall fight, the one of opinion, that he that thruſteth hath the vantage, and the other of opinion, that the warder hath the vantage, then most commonly the thruſter being valiant, with all ſpeed thruſteth home, and by reaſon of the time and ſwift motion of his hand, they are moſt commonly with the points of their rapiers, or daggers, or both, one or both of them hurt or ſlaine; becauſe their ſpaces of defence in that kind of fight, are too wide in due time to defend, and the place being wonne, the eye of the Patient by the ſwift motion of the Agents hand, is deceiued. Another reſolution they ſtand ſure vpon for their liues, to kill their enemies, in the which they are moſt commonly ſlaine themſelues: that is this: When they find the point of their enemies rapier out of the right line, they ſay, they may boldly make home a thruſt with a *Paſſata*, the which they obſerue, and do accordingly: but the other hauing a ſhorter time with his hand, as nature manie times teacheth him, ſodainly turneth his wriſt, whereby he meeteth the other in his paſſage iuſt with the point of his rapier in the face or body. And this falſe reſolution hath coſt manie a life.

That

That the cauſe that manie are ſo often ſlaine, and manie ſore hurt in fight with long Rapiers is not by reaſon of their dangerous thruſts, nor cunningneſſe of that Italienated fight, but in the length and vnweildineſſe thereof.

IT is moſt certaine, that men may with ſhort ſwords both ſtrike, thruſt, falſe and double, by reaſon of their diſtance and nimbleneſſe thereof, more dangerouſly then they can with long Rapiers: and yet when two fight with ſhort ſwordes, hauing true fight, there is no hurt done:neither is it poſſible in anie reaſon, that anie hurt ſhould be done betwixt them of either ſide, and this is well knowne to all ſuch as haue the perfection of true fight. By this it plainely appeareth, that the cauſe of the great ſlaughter, and ſundrie hurts done by long Rapiers, conſiſteth not in long Reach, dangerous thruſtes, nor cunningneſſe of the Italian fight, but in the inconuenient length, and vnweildineſſe of their long Rapiers: whereby it commonly falleth out, that in all their Actions appertaining to their defence, they are vnable, in due time to performe,and continually in danger of euerie croſſe, that ſhall happen to be made with their rapier blades, which being done, within the halfe rapier;(vnleſſe both be of one mind with all ſpeed to depart, which ſeldome or neuer happneth betweene men of valiant diſpoſition,)it is impoſſible to vncroſſe, or get out, or to auoid the ſtabbes of the Daggers. And this hath falne out manie times amongſt valiant men at thoſe weapons.

Of running and ſtanding faſt in Rapier fight, the runner hath the vantage.

6 IF two valiant men do fight being both cunning in running, & that they both vſe the ſame at one inſtant, their courſe is doubled, the place is wonne of both ſides, and one or both of them will commonly be ſlaine or ſore hurt: and if one of them ſhall runne, and the other ſtand faſt vpon the *Imbrocata* or *Stocata*, or howſoeuer, the place wilbe at one inſtant wonne of one ſide, and gained of the other, and one or both of them wilbe hurt or ſlaine: if both ſhall preſe hard vpon the guard, he that firſt thruſteth home in true place, hurteth the other: & if both thruſt together, they are both hurt: yet ſome vantage the runner hath, becauſe he is an vncertaine marke, and in his motion: the other is a certaine marke, and in a dead motion: and by reaſon thereof manie times the vnskilfull man taketh vantage he knoweth not how, againſt him that lyeth watching vpon his ward or *Stocata* guard.

Of ſtriking and thruſting both together.

7 It is ſtrongly holden of manie, that if in fight they find their enemy to haue more skill then themſelues, they preſently will continually ſtrike, & thruſt iuſt with him, whereby they will make their fight as good as his, and thereby haue as good aduantage as the other with all his skill: but if their ſwordes be longer then the other, then their aduantage is great; for it is certaine

certaine (ſay they) that an inch will kill a man: but if their ſwordes be much longer then the other, then their aduantage is ſo great, that they wilbe ſure by thruſting and ſtriking iuſt with the other, that they will alwaies hurt him that hath the ſhort ſword, and go cleare themſelues, becauſe they will reach him, when he ſhall not reach them. Theſe men ſpeake like ſuch as talke of Robin Hoode, that neuer ſhot in his bow; for to ſtrike or thruſt iuſt together with a man of skill, lyeth not in the will of the ignorant, becauſe the skilfull man alwaies fighteth vpon the true times, by the which the vnskilfull is ſtill diſappointed of both place and time, and therefore driuen of neceſſitie ſtill to watch the other, when & what he will doe; that is, whether he will ſtrike, thruſt, or falſe: if the vnskilfull ſtrike or thruſt in the time of falſing, therein he neither ſtriketh nor thruſteth iuſt with the other: he may ſaie, he hath ſtroke or thruſt before him, but not iuſt with him, nor to anie good purpoſe; for in the time of falſing, if he ſtrike or thruſt, he ſtriketh or thruſteth too ſhort: for in that time he hath neither time nor place to ſtrike home, and as it is ſaid, the vnskilfull man, that will take vpon him to ſtrike or thruſt iuſt with the skilfull, muſt firſt behold what the man of skil will doe, and when he will doe it, and therfore of neceſſitie is driuen to ſuffer the skilfull man to be the firſt mouer, and entred into his Action, whether it be blow or thruſt, the truth therof in reaſon cannot be denied. Now iudge whether it be poſſible for an vnskilfull man to ſtrike or thruſt iuſt together with a man of skill; but the skilfull man can moſt certainly ſtrike and thruſt iuſt together with the vnskilfull, becauſe the vnskilfull fighteth vpon falſe times, which being too long to anſwere the true times, the skilfull fighting vpon the true times, although the vnskilfull be the firſt mouer, & entred into his Action, whether it be blow or thruſt; yet the ſhortneſſe of the true times maketh at the pleaſure of the skilfull a iuſt meeting together: in perfect fight two neuer ſtrike or thruſt together, becauſe they neuer ſuffer place nor time to performe it.

Two vnskilfull men manie times by chance ſtrike and thruſte together, chance vnto them, becauſe they know not what they doe, or how it commeth to paſſe: but the reaſons or cauſes be theſe. Sometimes two falſe times meet & make a iuſt time together, & ſometimes a true time and a falſe time meeteth and maketh a iuſt time together, and ſometimes two true times meet and make a iuſt time together. And all this hapneth becauſe the true time and place is vnknowne vnto them.

George Siluer his reſolution vpon that hidden or doubtfull queſtion, who hath the aduantage of the Offender or Defender.

The aduantage is ſtrongly holden of many to be in the offender, yea in ſomuch, that if two minding to offend in their fight, it is thought to be in him that firſt ſtriketh or thruſteth. Others ſtrongly hold opinion that the wardr abſolutely hath ſtill the aduantage, but theſe opinions as they are contrary the one to the other: ſo are they contrarie to true fight, as may well be ſeene by theſe ſhort examples. If the aduantage be in the warder, then it is not good anie time to ſtrike or thruſt: if the aduantage be in the ſtriker or thruſter, then were it a friuolous a friuolous thing to learne to ward, or at anie time to ſeeke to ward, ſince in warding lieth diſaduantage. Now may it plainly by theſe examples appeare, that if there be anie perfection in fight, that both ſides are deceiued in their opinions, becauſe if the ſtriker or thruſter haue the aduantage, then is the warder ſtill in danger of wounds or death. And againe, if the warder hath the aduantage, then is the ſtriker or thruſter in as great daunger to defend himſelfe againſt the warder, becauſe the warder from his wards, taketh aduantage of the ſtriker or thruſter vpon euerie blow or thruſt, that ſhall be made againſt him. Then thus I conclude, that if there be perfection in the Science of Defence, they are all in their opinons deceiued; and that the truth may appeare for the ſatisfaction of all men, this is my reſolution: there is no aduantage abſolutely, nor diſaduantage in ſtriker, thruſter, or warder: and there is a great aduantage in the ſtriker thruſter & warder: but in this maner, in the perfection of fight the aduantage conſiſteth in fight betweene partie and partie: that is, whoſoeuer winneth or gaineth the place in true pace, ſpace and time, hath the aduantage, whether he be ſtriker, thruſter or warder. And that is my reſolution.

Of Spanish fight vvith the Rapier.

THe *Spaniard* is now thought to be a better 9
man with his Rapier then is the Italian, Frenchman, high Almaine, or anie other countrie man whatſoeuer, becauſe they in their Rapier-fight ſtand vpon ſo manie intricate trickes,

that in all the courſe of a mans life it ſhall be hard to learne them, and if they miſſe in doing the leaſt of them in their fight, they are in danger of death. But the *Spaniard* in his fight, both ſafely to defend himſelfe, and to endanger his enemie, hath but one onely lying, and two wards to learne, wherein a man with ſmall practiſe in a verie ſhort time may become perfect.

This is the maner of Spaniſh fight, they ſtand as braue as they can with their bodies ſtraight vpright, narrow ſpaced, with their feet continually mouing, as if they were in a dance, holding forth their armes and Rapiers verie ſtraight againſt the face or bodies of their enemies: & this is the only lying to accompliſh that kind of fight. And this note, that as long as any man ſhall lie in that maner with his arme, and point of his Rapier ſtraight, it ſhall be impoſſible for his aduerſarie to hurt him, becauſe in that ſtraight holding forth of his arme, which way ſoeuer a blow ſhall be made againſt him, by reaſon that his Rapier hilt lyeth ſo farre before him, he hath but a verie litle way to moue, to make his ward perfect, in this maner. If a blow be made at the right ſide of the head, a verie litle mouing of the hand with the knuckles vpward defendeth that ſide of the head or bodie, and the point being ſtill out ſtraight, greatly endangereth the ſtriker: and ſo likewiſe, if a blow be made at the left ſide of the head, a verie ſmall turning of the wriſt with the knuckles downward, defendeth that ſide of the head and bodie, and the point of the Rapier much indangereth the hand, arme, face or bodie of the ſtriker: and if anie thruſt be made, the wards, by reaſon of the indirections in mouing the feet in maner of dauncing, as aforeſaid, maketh a perfect ward, and ſtill withall the

point

point greatly endangereth the other. And thus is the Spaniſh fight perfect: ſo long as you can keepe that order, and ſoone learned, and therefore to be accounted the beſt fight with the Rapier of all other. But note how this Spaniſh fight is perfect, and you ſhall ſee no longer then you can keepe your point ſtraight againſt your aduerſarie: as for example, I haue heard the like ieſt.

There was a cunning Doctor at his firſt going to ſea, being doubtfull that he ſhould be ſea-ſicke, an old woman perceiuing the ſame, ſaid vnto him: Sir, I pray, be of good comfort, I will teach you a tricke to auoid that doubt; here is a fine pibble ſtone, if you pleaſe to accept it, take it with you, and when you be on ſhip-bord, put it in your mouth, and as long as you ſhall keepe the ſame in your mouth, vpon my credit you ſhall neuer vomit: the Doctor beleeued her, and tooke it thankfully at her hands, and when he was at ſea, he began to be ſicke, whereupon he preſently put the ſtone in his mouth, & there kept it ſo long as he poſſibly could, but through his extreme ſickneſſe the ſtone with vomit was caſt out of his mouth: then preſently he remẽbred how the woman had mocked him, and yet her words were true.

Euen ſo a *Spaniard* hauing his Rapier point put by, may receiue a blow on the head, or a cut ouer the face, hand, or arme, or a thruſt in the body or face, and yet his Spaniſh fight perfect, ſo long as he can keepe ſtraight the point of his Rapier againſt the face or body of his aduerſarie: which is as eaſie in that maner of fight to be done, as it was for the Doctor in the extremity of his vomite to keepe the ſtone in his mouth.

Yet one other pretie ieſt more, ſcarce worth the reading, in commendation of outlandiſh fight. There was an *Italian* teacher of Defence in my time, who was ſo excellent in his fight, that he would haue hit anie Engliſh man with a thruſt, iuſt vpon any button in his doublet, and this was much ſpoken of.

Alſo there was another cunning man in catching of wildgeeſe, he would haue made no more ado, when he had heard them crie, as the maner of wildgeeſe is, flying one after another in rowes, but preſently looking vp, would tell them, if there had bene a doſen, ſixteene, twẽtie, or more, he would haue taken euerie one. And this tale was manie times told by men of good credit, and much maruelled at by the hearers: & the man that wold haue taken the wildgeeſe, was of good credite himſelfe: marie they ſaid, indeed he did neuer take anie, but at anie time when he had looked vp, and ſeene them flie in that maner, he would with all his heart haue taken thẽ, but he could no more tell how to do it, then could the cunning *Italian* Fencer tell how to hit an Engliſhman, with a thruſt iuſt vpon any one of his buttons, when he liſted.

Illuſions for the maintenance of imperfect weapons & falſe fights, to feare or diſcourage the vnskilfull in their weapons, from taking a true courſe or vſe, for attaining to the perfect knowledge of true fight.

10 First, for the Rapier (ſaith the *Italian*, or falſe teacher) I hold it to be a perfect good weapõ, becauſe the croſſe hindreth not to hold the handle in the hand, to thruſt both far & ſtraight, & to vſe all maner of aduantages in the wards,

or

or ſodainly to caſt the ſame at the aduerſarie, but with the Sword you are driuen with all the ſtrength of the hand to hold faſt the handle. And in the warres I would wiſh no friend of mine to weare Swords with hilts, becauſe when they are ſodainly ſet vpon, for haſte they ſet their hands vpon their hilts in ſteed of their handles: in which time it hapneth manie times before they can draw their ſwords, they are ſlaine by their enemies. And for Sword and Buckler fight, it is imperfect, becauſe the buckler blindeth the ſight, neither would I haue anie man lie aloft with his hand aboue his head, to ſtrike ſound blowes. Strong blowes are naught, eſpecially being ſet aboue the head, becauſe therein all the face and bodie is diſcouered. Yet I confeſſe, in old times, when blowes were only vſed with ſhort Swords & Bucklers,& back Sword, theſe kind of fights were good & moſt mãly, but now in theſe daies fight is altered. Rapiers are lõger for aduãtage thẽ ſwords were wõt to be: whẽ blowes were vſed, men were ſo ſimple in their fight, that they thought him to be a coward, that wold make a thruſt or ſtrike a blow beneath the girdle. Againe, if their weapõs were ſhort, as in times paſt they were, yet fight is better looked into in theſe dayes, than then it was. Who is it in theſe daies ſeeth not that the blow cõpaſſeth round like a wheele, whereby it hath a longer way to go, but the thruſt paſſeth in a ſtraight line, and therefore commeth a nearer way, and done in a ſhorter time thẽ is the blow, and is more deadly then is the blow? Therefore there is no wiſe man that will ſtrike, vnleſſe he be wearie of his life. It is certaine, that the point for aduantage euerie way in fight is to be vſed, the blow is vtterly naught, and not to be vſed. He that fighteth vpon the

Theſe counterfeit ſhews are enough to cary the wiſeſt that know not the true fight frõ the falſe, out of the right way.

And if their weapons were ſhort, as in times paſt they were, yet they could not thruſt ſafe at body or face, becauſe in gardant fight they fall ouer, or vnder the perfect croſſe of the ſword & to ſtrike beneath the waſte, or at the legges, is great diſaduantage, becauſe the courſe of the blow to the legs is too far, & therby the head, face, & body is diſcouered: and that was the cauſe in old time, that they did not thruſt nor ſtrike at the legs, & not for lacke of skill, as in theſe daies we imagine. Againe, if a man in thoſe daies ſhold haue fought with a long ſword, they would preſently haue put him into Gobbes Trauers.

blow eſpecially with a ſhort ſword, wilbe ſore hurt or ſlaine. The deuill can ſay no more for the maintenance of errors.

That a blow commeth continually as neare a way as a thruſt, and moſt commonly nearer, ſtronger, more ſwifter, and is ſooner done.

11 *A confutation of their errours.*

THe blow, by reaſō that it compaſſeth round like a wheele, whereby it hath a longer way to come, as the Italian Fenſer ſaith, & that the thruſt paſſing in a ſtraight line, commeth a nearer way, and therefore is ſooner done then a blow, is not true: these be the proofes.

Let two lie in their perfect ſtrengths and readineſſe, wherein the blades of their Rapiers by the motion of the body, may not be croſſed of either ſide, the one to ſtrike, and the other to thruſt. Then meaſure the diſtance or courſe wherein the hand and hilt paſſeth to finiſh the blow of the one, and the thruſt of the other, and you ſhall find them both by meaſure, in diſtance all one. And let anie man of iudgement being ſeene in the exerciſe of weapons, not being more addicted vnto nouelties of fight, then vnto truth it ſelfe, put in meaſure, and practiſe theſe three fights, variable, open, and guardant, and he ſhall ſee, that whenſoeuer anie man lyeth at the thruſt vpon the variable fight, (where of neceſſitie moſt commonly he lyeth, or otherwiſe not poſſiblie to keepe his Rapier from croſſing at the blow & thruſt, vpon the open or gardant fight,) that the blowes & thruſtes from theſe two fightes, come a nearer way, and a more ſtronger

ſtronger and ſwifter courſe then doth the thruſt, out of the variable fight. And thus for a generall rule, whereſoeuer the Thruſter lyeth, or out of what fight ſoeuer he fighteth, with his Rapier, or Rapier and Dagger, the blow in his courſe commeth as neare, and nearer, and more ſwift and ſtronger then doth the thruſt.

Perfect fight ſtandeth vpon both blow and thruſt, therefore the thruſt is not onely to be vſed.

THat there is no fight perfect without both blow and thruſt: neither is there anie certaine rule to be ſet downe for the vſe of the point onely, theſe be the reaſons: In fight there are manie motions, with the hand, bodie, and feet, and in euerie motion the place of the hand is altered, & becauſe by the motions of the hand, the altering of the places of the hand, the changes of lyings, wards, and breaking of thruſtes, the hand will ſometimes be in place to ſtrike, ſome times to thruſt, ſometimes after a blow to thruſt, and ſometimes after a thruſt to ſtrike, & ſometimes in place where you may ſtrike, and cannot thruſt without loſſe of time, and ſometimes in place where you may thruſt, and cannot ſtrike without loſſe of time, and ſometimes in place where you can neither ſtrike nor thruſt, vnleſſe you fight vpon both blow and thruſt, nor able to defend your ſelfe by ward or going backe, becauſe your ſpace wilbe too wide, and your diſtance loſt. And ſometimes when you haue made a thruſt, a ward or breaking is taken in ſuch ſort with the Dagger or blade of the Sword, that you cã neither thruſt againe, nor defend your ſelfe vnleſſe you do ſtrike, which 12

This in truth cannot be denied.

you may ſoundly doe, and go free, and ſometimes when you ſtrike, a ward wilbetaken in ſuch ſort, that you cannot ſtrike againe, nor defend your ſelfe, vnleſſe you thruſt, which you may ſafely doe and goe free. So to conclude, there is no perfection in the true fight, without both blow and thruſt, nor certaine rule to be ſet downe for the point onely.

That the blow is more dangerous and deadly in fight, then a thruſt, for proofe thereof to be made according with Art, an Engliſhman holdeth argument againſt an Italian.

Italian.

13 WHich is more dangerous or deadly in fight of a blow or a thruſt?

Engliſhman.

This queſtion is not propounded according to art, becauſe there is no fight perfect without both blow and thruſt.

Italian.

Let it be ſo, yet opinions are otherwiſe holden, that the thruſt is onely to be vſed, becauſe it commeth a nearer way, and is more dangerous and deadly, for theſe reaſons: firſt the blow compaſſeth round like a wheele, but the thruſt paſſeth in a ſtraight line, therfore the blow by reaſon of the compaſſe, hath a longer way to go then the thruſt, & is therefore longer in doing, but the thruſt paſſeth in a ſtraight line, therfore hath ſhorter way to go thẽ hath the blow, & is therfore done in a ſhorter time, & is therfore much better then the blow, & more dangerous and deadly, becauſe if a thruſt do hit the face or bodie, it indangereth life, and moſt commonly death enſueth; but if the blow hit the bodie, it is not ſo dãgerous.

Engliſhman.

Englishman.

Let your opiniōs be what they wil, but that the thrust cōmeth a nearer way, & is sooner done then the blow, is not true: & for proofe thereof reade the twelfth Paradox. And now will I set downe probable reasons, that the blow is better then the thrust, and more dangerous and deadly. First, the blow commeth as neare a way, & most cōmonly nearer then doth the thrust, & is therfore done in a shorter time then is the thrust: therfore in respect of time, wherupon stādeth the perfection of fight, the blow is much better then the thrust. Againe, the force of the thrust passeth straight, therefore any crosse being indirectly made, the force of a child may put it by: but the force of a blow passeth indirectly, therefore must be directly warded in the countercheck of his force: which cānot be done but by the couenient strength of a man, & with true crosse in true time, or else will not safely defēd him: and is therfore much better, & more dāgerous thē the thrust, and againe, the thrust being made through the hand, arme, or leg, or in many places of the body and face, are not deadly, neither are they maimes, or losse of limmes or life, neither is he much hindred for the time in his fight, as long as the bloud is hot:for example.

The blow more dangerous then the thrust.

I haue knowne a Gētlemā hurt in Rapier fight, in nine or ten places through the bodie, armes, and legges, and yet hath continued in his fight, & afterward hath slaine the other, and come home and hath bene cured of all his woūds without maime, & is yet liuing. But the blow being strōgly made, taketh somtimes cleane away the hand from the arme, hath manie times bene seene. Againe, a full blow vpon the head or face with a short sharpe Sword, is most commonly death. A full blow vpon the

The blow cutteth off the hand, the arme, the leg, and sometimes the head.

necke, ſhoulder, arme, or legge, indangereth life, cutteth off the veines, muſcles, and ſinewes, periſheth the bones: theſe wounds made by the blow, in reſpect of perfect healing, are the loſſe of limmes, or maimes incurable for euer.

And yet more for the blow: a ful blow vpon the head, face, arme, leg, or legs, is death, or the partie so wounded in the mercie of him that ſhall ſo wound him. For what man ſhall be able long in fight to ſtand vp, either to reuenge, or defend himſelfe, hauing the veines, muſcles, and ſinewes of his hand, arme, or leg cleane cut aſunder? or being diſmembred by ſuch wound vpon the face or head, but ſhall be enforced therby, and through the loſſe of bloud, the other a litle dallying with him, to yeeld himſelf, or leaue his life in his mercie?

He that giueth the firſt wound with a ſtrong blow, commaundeth the life of the other.

And for plainer deciding this cõtrouerſie betweene the blow and the thruſt, conſider this ſhort note. The blow commeth manie wayes, the thruſt doth not ſo. The blow commeth a nearer way then a thruſt moſt commonly, and is therefore ſooner done. The blow requireth the ſtrength of a man to be warded; but the thruſt may be put by, by the force of a child. A blow vpon the hand, arme, or legge is a maime incurable; but a thruſt in the hand, arme, or legge is to be recouered. The blow hath manie parts to wound, and in euerie of them commaundeth the life; but the thruſt hath but a few, as the bodie or face, and not in euerie part of them neither.

Of

Of the difference betwixt the true fight & the falſe: wherin conſiſteth (the Principles being had with the direction of the foure Gouernors) the whole perfection of fight with all maner of weapons.

THe true fights be theſe: whatſoeuer is done with the hand before the foot or feet is true fight. The falſe fights be theſe: whatſoeuer is done with the foot or feet before the hand, is falſe, becauſe the hand is ſwifter then the foot, the foot or feet being a ſlower mouer then the hand: the hand in that maner of fight is tied to the time of the foot or feet, and being tied thereto, hath loſt his freedome, and is made thereby as ſlow in his motions as the foot or feet: and therfor that fight is falſe. 14

Of euill orders or cuſtomes in our English Fēce-ſchooles, & of the old or ancient teaching of weapons, & things very neceſſarie to be continued for the auoiding of errors, and reuiuing and continuance of our ancient vveapons, and moſt victorious fight againe.

THere is in my opiniō in our Fence-ſchooles an euill order or cuſtome in theſe dayes vſed, the which, if it might ſtand with the good liking of our Maiſters of Defence, I thinke it neceſſarie to be left: for as long as it is vſed, it ſhall be hard to make a good Scholler. 15

That is this, at the ſingle Sword, Sword and Dagger, & Sword and Buckler, they forbid the thruſt, & at the ſingle Rapier, and Rapier & Dagger, they forbid the blow. Either they are both together beſt, or the thruſt altogether beſt, or the blow altogether beſt. If the thruſt be beſt, why do we not vſe it at the ſingle Sword, Sword & Dagger, & Sword and Buckler. If the blow be beſt, why do we not vſe it at the ſingle Rapier, Rapier & Poinyard? But knowing by the Art of Armes, that no fight is perfect without both blow and thruſt, why do we not vſe and teach both blow and thruſt? But howſoeuer this we dayly ſee, that whẽ two meet in fight, whether they haue skill or none, vnleſſe ſuch as haue tied thẽſelues to that boyiſh, *Italian*, weake, imperfect fight, they both ſtrike and thruſt, and how ſhall he then do, that being much taught in ſchoole, neuer learned to ſtrike, nor how to defend a ſtrong blow? & how ſhall he thẽ do, that being brought vp in Fẽce-ſchoole, that neuer learned to thruſt with the ſingle Sword, Sword and Dagger, and Sword and Buckler, nor how at theſe weapõs to breake a thruſt? Surely, I thinke a downe right fellow, that neuer came in ſchoole, vſing ſuch skill as nature yeeldeth out of his courage, ſtrength, and agilitie, with good downe right blowes and thruſts among, as ſhall beſt frame in his hands, ſhold put one of theſe imperfect ſchollers greatly to his ſhifts. Beſides, there are now in theſe dayes no gripes, cloſes, wreſtlings, ſtriking with the hilts, daggers, or bucklers, vſed in Fence-ſchooles. Our ploughmen by nature wil do all theſe things with great ſtrẽgth & agility: but the Schooleman is altogether vnacquainted with theſe things. He being faſt tyed to ſuch ſchoolplay as he hath learned, hath loſt thereby the benefite

of

of nature, and the plowman is now by nature without art a farre better man then he. Therefore in my opinion, as long as we barre anie maner of play in ſchoole, we ſhall hardly make a good ſcholler: there is no maner of teaching comparable to the old ancient teaching, that is, firſt their quarters, then their wardes, blowes, thruſts, and breaking of thruſtes, then their Cloſes and Gripes, ſtriking with the hilts, Daggers, Bucklers, Wraſtlings, ſtriking with the foote or knee in the Coddes, and all theſe are ſafely defended in learning perfectly of the Gripes. And this is the ancient teaching, the perfecteſt & moſt beſt teaching; and without this teaching, there ſhall neuer ſcholler be made able, doe his vttermoſt, nor fight ſafe. Againe their ſwordes in ſchooles are too long by almoſt halfe a foote to vncroſſe, without going backe with the feete, within diſtance or perfectly to ſtrike or thruſt within the halfe or quarter ſword. And in ſeruing of the Prince, when men do meet together in publique fight, are vtterly naught and vnſeruiceable. The beſt lengthes for perfect teaching of the true fight to be vſed and continued in Fence ſchooles, to accord with the true ſtatures of all men, are theſe. The blade to be a yard and an inch for meane ſtatures, and for men of tall ſtatures, a yard and three or foure inches, and no more. And I would haue the Rapier continued in ſchooles, alwaies readie for ſuch as ſhall thinke themſelues cunning, or ſhall haue delight to play with that imperfect weapon. Prouided alwaies, that the Schoolemaiſter or Vſher play with him with his ſhort Sword, plying him with all maner of fight according to the true art: this being continued the truth ſhall flouriſh, the lye ſhalbe beaten downe, and all nations not ha-

In the warres there is no obſeruation of Stoccatas, Imbrocatas, times, nor anſwers.

Long weapons imperfect.

uing the true ſcience, ſhall come with all gladneſſe to the valiant and moſt braue Engliſh maisters of Defence to learne the true fight for their defence.

16 *The grounds or Principles of true fight with all maner of weapons.*

FIrſt Judgement, Lyings, Diſtance, Direction, Paſe, Space, Place, Time, Indirection, Motion, Action, generall and continuall Motion, Progreſſion, Regreſſion, Trauerſing, and Treading of groundes, Blowes, Thruſtes, Faulſes, Doubles, Slipes, Wardes, breakings of Thruſts, Cloſings, Gripes, & Wraſtlings, Guardant fight, Open fight, Variable fight, and Cloſe fight, and foure Gouernours.

The wardes of all maner of weapons.

17 AL ſingle weapons haue foure wardes, and all double weapons haue eight wardes. The ſingle ſword hath two with the point vp, and two with the point downe. The Staffe and all maner of weapons to be vſed with both handes haue the like.

The Sword and Buckler, and Sword and Dagger are double weapons, and haue eight wardes, two with the point vp, and two with the point downe, and two for the legges with the point downe, the point to be caried for both ſides of the legges, with the knuckles downeward, and two wardes with the Dagger or Buckler for the head. The Forreſt bill is a double weapon by reaſon of of the head, and therefore hath eight wardes, foure with the Staffe, foure with the head, foure of them to be vſed as with the ſtaffe, and the other foure with the head, the one vp, the other downe, and the other ſidewaies.

The names and numbers of times appertaining vnto fight bothtrue and falſe.

THere are eight times, whereof foure are true, and foure are falſe: the true times be theſe. 18

The time of the hand.

The time of the hand and bodie.

The time of the hand, bodie and foote.

The time of the hand, bodie and feete.

The falſe times be theſe.

The time of the foote.

The time of the foote and bodie.

The time of the foote, bodie and hand.

The time of the feete, bodie and hand.

Thus haue I thought good to ſeparate and make knowne the true times from the falſe, with the true wardes thereto belonging, that thereby the rather in practiſing of weapons, a true courſe may be taken for the auoiding of errours and euill cuſtomes, and ſpeedie attaining of good habit or perfect being in the true vſe and knowledge of all maner of weapons.

Of the length of weapons, and how euerie man may fit himſelfe in the perfect length of his weapon, according to his owne ſtature, with briefe reaſons wherefore they ought to be ſo.

19 TO know the perfect length of your Sword, you shall stand with your sword and dagger drawn, as you see this picture, keeping out straight your dagger arme, drawinge backe your sword as far as conueniently you can, not opening the elbow ioynt of your sword arme: and looke what you can draw within your dagger, that is the iust length of your sword, to be made according to your owne stature.

If the sword be longer, you can hardly vncrosse without going backe with your feet. If shorter, thē you can hardly make a true crosse without putting in of your feet, the which times are too long to answer the time of the hand.

The like reasons for the short staffe, half Pike, Forrest bill, Partisan, or Gleue, or such like weapons of perfect length.

The perfect length of your two hand ſword is, the blade to be the length of the blade of your ſingle ſword.

To know the perfect length of your ſhort ſtaffe, or half Pike, Forreſt bil, Partiſan, or Gleue, or ſuch like weapons of vantage and perfect lengths, you ſhall ſtand vpright, holding the ſtaffe vpright cloſe by your body, with your left hãd, reaching with your right hand your ſtaffe as high as you can, and then allow to that length a ſpace to ſet both your hands, when you come to fight, wherein you may conueniently ſtrike, thruſt, and ward, & that is the iuſt length to be made according to your ſtature. And this note, that theſe lengths will commonly fall out to be eight or nine foot long, and will fit, although not iuſt, the ſtatures of all men, without any hindrance at all vnto them in their fight, becauſe in any weapon wherin the hands may be remoued, and at libertie, to make the weapon lõger or ſhorter in fight at his pleaſure, a foot of the ſtaffe behind the backmoſt hand doth no harme. And wherfore theſe weapons ought to be of the lengths aforeſaid, and no ſhorter, theſe are the reaſons: If they ſhould be ſhorter, then the long ſtaffe, Morris Pike, and ſuch like weapons ouer and aboue the perfect length, ſhould haue great vantage againſt them, becauſe he may come boldly and ſafe without anie gard or ward, to the place where he may thruſt home, and at euery thruſt put him in danger of his life: but if theſe weapons be of their perfect lengths, then can the long ſtaffe, the Morris Pike, or anie other longer weapon ly nowhere in true ſpace, but ſhall be ſtill within compaſſe of the croſſe, to croſſe and vncroſſe, wherby he may ſafely paſſe home to the place, where he may ſtrike or thruſt him that hath the long weapon, in the head, face, or body at his pleaſure.

Of the lengths of the Battel axe, Halbard, or blacke Bill, or ſuch like vveapons of weight, appertaining vnto gard or battell.

20 IN anie of theſe weapons there needeth no iuſt length, but commonly they are, or ought to be fiue or ſixe foot long, & may not well be vſed much longer, becauſe of their weights: and being weapons for the warres or battell, when men are ioyned cloſe together, may thruſt, & ſtrike ſound blowes, with great force both ſtrong and quicke: and finally for the iuſt lengths of all other ſhorter or longer weapons to be gouerned with both hands, there is none: neither is there anie certaine lengthes in anie maner of weapons to be vſed with one hand, ouer or vnder the iuſt length of the ſingle ſword.

Thus endeth the length of weapons.

Of the vantages of weapons in their kinds, places, & times, both in priuate and publike fight.

21 FIrſt I will begin with the worſt weapon, an imperfect and inſufficient weapon, and not worth the ſpeaking of; but now being highly eſteemed, therefore not to be left vnremembred; that is, the ſingle Rapier, and Rapier and Poiniard.

The ſingle Sword hath the vantage againſt the ſingle Rapier.

The Sword and Dagger hath the vantage againſt the Rapier and Poiniard.

The

The Sword & Target hath aduātage againſt the Sword and Dagger, or Rapier and Poiniard.

The Sword and Buckler hath aduantage againſt the Sword and Target, the Sword and Dagger, or Rapier and Poiniard.

The two hand Sword, hath the vantage againſt the Sword and Target, the Sword and Buckler, the Sword and Dagger, or Rapier and Poiniard.

The Battel-axe, the Halbard, the Blacke-bill, or ſuch like weapons of weight, appertaining vnto guard or battell, are all one in fight, and haue aduantage againſt the two hand Sword, the Sword and Buckler, the Sword and Target, the Sword & dagger, or the Rapier & Poiniard.

The ſhort ſtaffe or halfe Pike, Forreſt-bill, Partiſan, or Gleue, or ſuch like weapons of perfect length, haue the vantage againſt the Battel-axe, the Halbard, the Blacke-bill, the two hand ſword, the Sword and Target, and are too hard for two Swords and Daggers, or two Rapiers and Poiniards with Gantlets, and for the long ſtaffe and Morris Pike.

The long Staffe, Morris Pike, or Iauelin, or ſuch like weapons aboue the perfect length, haue aduantage againſt all maner of weapons, the ſhort ſtaffe, Welch hooke, Partiſan, or Gleue, or ſuch like weapons of vantage excepted: yet too weake for two Swords and Daggers or two Swords and Bucklers, or two Rapiers and Poiniards with Gantlets, becauſe they are too long to thruſt, ſtrike, and turne ſpeedily: and by reaſon of the large diſtance, one of the Sword and Dagger-men will get behind him.

The Welch hooke or Forreſt bill, hath aduantage againſt all maner of weapons whatſoeuer.

Yet vnderſtand, that in battels, and where varietie of weapons be, amongſt multitudes of men and horſes, the Sword and Target, the two hand Sword, the Battel-axe, the Blacke-bill, and Halbard, are better weapons, and more dangerous in their offence and forces, then is the Sword and Buckler, ſhort ſtaffe, long ſtaffe, or Forreſt bill. The Sword and Target leadeth vpon Shot, and in troupes defendeth thruſts and blowes giuen by battel-axe, Halbards, Blacke-bill, or two hand ſwords, far better then can the Sword and Buckler.

The Morris Pike defendeth the battell from both horſe and man, much better then can the ſhort ſtaffe, long ſtaffe, or Forreſt bill. Againe, the Battel-axe, the Halbard, the Blacke bill, the two hand ſword, and Sword & Target, amongſt armed men and troopes, when men are come together, by reaſon of their weights, ſhortneſſe, and great forces, do much more offend the enemie, & are then much better weapons, then is the ſhort ſtaffe, the long Staffe, or Forreſt bill.

Of the inſufficiencie and diſaduantages of the Rapiers-fight in Battell.

22 FOr the ſingle Rapier, or Rapier & Poiniard, they are imperfect & inſufficient weapons: and eſpecially in the ſeruice of the Prince, when men ſhall ioyne together, what ſeruice can a ſouldier do with a Rapier, a childiſh toy wherwith a man can do nothing but thruſt, nor that neither, by reaſon of the length, and in euerie mouing when blowes are a dealing, for lacke of a hilt is in daunger to haue his hand or arme cut off, or his head

clouen ?

clouen . And for Wardes and Gripes, they haue none, neither can any of theſe fine Rapier men, for lacke of vſe, tell howe to ſtrike a ſound blow.

Of the vantages and ſufficiencie of the short Sword fight in battell.

THe ſhort Sword, and Sword and Dagger, 23
are perfect good weapons, and eſpecially in ſeruice of the Prince. What a braue weapon is a ſhort ſharpe light Sword, to carie, to draw, to be nimble withall, to ſtrike, to cut, to thruſt both ſtrong and quicke. And what a goodly defence is a ſtrong ſingle hilt, when men are cluſtering and hurling together, eſpecially where varietie of weapons be, in their motions to defend the hand, head, face, and bodies, from blowes, that ſhalbe giuen ſometimes with Swordes, ſometimes with two handed Swordes, battell Axe, Halbardes, or blacke Billes, and ſometimes men ſhalbe ſo neare together, that they ſhall haue no ſpace, ſcarce to vſe the blades of their Swordes belowe their waſtes, then their hilts (their handes being aloft) defendeth from the blowes, their handes, armes, heads, faces, and bodies: then they lay on, hauing the vſe of blowes and Gripes, by force of their armes with their hilts, ſtrong blowes, at the head, face, armes, bodies, and ſhoulders, and manie times in hurling together, ſcope is giuen to turne downe their points, with violent thruſts at their faces, and bodies, by reaſon of the ſhortneſſe of their blades, to the mightie annoyance, diſcomfort, and great deſtruction of their enimies. One valiant man with a Sword in his hand, will doe better ſeruice, then ten *Italians*, or Italienated with the Rapiers.

That all maner of double weapons, or weapons to be vſed with both handes, haue aduantage againſt the ſingle Rapier or ſingle Sword, there is no queſtion to be made.

That the Sword and Buckler hath the vantage againſt the Sword and Dagger.

24 THe Dagger is an imperfect ward, although borne out ſtraight, to make the Space narrow, whereby by a litle mouing of the hand, may be ſufficient to ſaue both ſides of the head, or to breake the thruſt from the face or body, yet for lacke of the circumference his hand will lie too high or too low, or too weake, to defend both blow and thruſt: if he lye ſtraight with narrow ſpace, which is beſt to breake the thruſt, then he lieth too weake, and too lowe to defend his head from a ſtrong blow: if he lye high, that is ſtrong to defend his head, but then his ſpace wilbe too wide to breake the thruſt from his bodie. The Dagger ſerueth well at length to put by a thruſt, and at the halfe Sword to croſſe the Sword blade, to driue out the Agent, and put him in danger of his life, and ſafely in anie of theſe two actions to defend himſelfe. But the Buckler, by reaſon of his circumference and weight, being well caried, defendeth ſafely in all times and places, whether it be at the point, halfe Sword, the head, bodie, and face, from all maner of blowes and thruſtes whatſoeuer, yet I haue heard manie hold opinion, that the Sword and Dagger hath aduantage of the Sword and Buckler, at the Cloſe, by reaſon of the length and point of the Dagger: and at the point

point of the Sword, they can better ſee to ward then with a Buckler. But I neuer knew anie, that wanne the Cloſe with the Dagger vpon the Sword and Budkler, but did wiſh himſelfe out againe:for diſtance being broken, iudgement faileth, for lacke of time to iudge, and the eie is deceiued by the ſwift motion of the hand, and for lacke of true Space with the dagger hand, which cannot be otherwiſe, for lacke of the circumference to defend both blow and thruſt, it is impoſſible for lacke ot true Space in iuſt time, the agent hauing gotten the true place, to defend one thruſt or blow of an hundred. And it is moſt certaine, whoſoeuer cloſeth with Sword and Dagger, againſt the Sword and Buckler, is in great danger to be ſlaine. Likewiſe at the point within diſtance, if he ſtand to defend both blow and thruſt with his Dagger, for lacke of true ſpace and diſtance, if he had the beſt eye of anie man, and could ſee perfectly, which way the thruſt or blow commeth, and when it commeth, as it is not to be denied but he may, yet his ſpace being too large, it helpeth him nothing, becauſe one mans hand being as ſwift as another mans hand, both being within diſtance, he that ſtriketh or thruſteth, hurteth the warder: the reaſon is this: the Agent being in the firſt motion although in his offence, further to go then the warder to defend, yet the warders ſpace being too large, the blow or thruſt wilbe performed home, before the warder can come to the true plaee to defend himſelfe, and although the warder doe perfectly ſee the blow or thruſt comming, ſo ſhall he ſee his owne ward ſo farre from the true place of his defence, that although he doe at that inſtant time, plainly ſee the blow or thruſt comming, it ſhalbe impoſſible for him to recouer the true place of his ward, till he be wounded. But let the warder with the dagger ſay, that it is not true which I haue ſaid, for as he hath eies to behold the blow or thruſt cōming, ſo hath he as good time to defend himſelf. Herein he ſhal find himſelf deceiued to; this is the reaſon: the hand is the ſwifteſt motion, the foot is the ſloweſt, without diſtance the hand is tied to the motion of the feet, wherby the time of the hand is made as ſlow as the foot, becauſe thereby we redeeme euerie time loſt vpon his comming by the ſlow motion of the foot, & haue time therby to iudge, whē & how he can performe any actiō whatſoeuer, and ſo haue we the time of the hand to the time of the feet. Now is the hād in his owne courſe more ſwifter then the foot or eye, therfore within diſtance the eye is deceiued, & iudgement is loſt; and that is another cauſe that the warder with the dagger, although he haue perfect eyes, is ſtil within diſtance deceiued. For proofe that the hand is more ſwifter then the eye, & thereby deceiueth the eyes: let two ſtand within diſtance, & let one of thē ſtand ſtill to defend himſelf, & let the other floriſh & falſe with his hand, and he ſhall continually with the ſwift motions of his hand, deceiue the eyes of him that ſtandeth watching to defend himſelfe, & ſhal continually ſtrike him in diuerſe places with his hand. Againe, take this for an example, that the eyes by ſwift motions are deceiued: turne a turne-wheele ſwift, & you ſhall not be able to diſcerne with your beſt eies how many ſpokes be in the wheele, no nor whether there be any ſpokes at all, or whereof the wheele is made, and yet you ſee when the wheele ſtandeth ſtill there is a large diſtance betweene euerie ſpoke. He that will not beleeue that the ſwift motion of the hand in fight will deceiue the eye, ſhal ſtare abroad

The eye is deceiued by the ſwift motion of the hād.

broad with his eyes,& feele himſelf ſoundly hurt,before he ſhall perfectly ſee how to defend himſelfe. So thoſe that truſt to their ſight,the excellẽcy of a good eye,their great cunning, & perfect wards of the daggers,that they can better ſee to ward then with a buckler,ſhall euer be deceiued. And whẽ they be wounded,they ſay the Agẽt was a litle too quicke for them;ſometimes they ſay they bare their dagger a litle too low : ſometimes they are thruſt vnder the dagger,then they ſay,they bare it a litle too high :ſometimes a thruſt being ſtrongly made , they being ſoundly paid therewith, ſay, they were a litle too ſlow,& ſometimes they be ſoundly paid with a thruſt,& they thinke they were a litle too quick. So they that practiſe or thinke to be cunning in the dagger ward, are all the dayes of their liues learning,and are neuer taught.

The Dagger is an imperfect ward.

That the Sword and Buckler hath the vantage against the Sword and Target.

THe Sword & Target together hath but two 25
fights;that is, the variable fight, & the cloſe fight,for the cloſe fight, the nũber of his feet are too many to take againſt any mã of skill hauing the Sword & buckler,& for the variable fight although not ſo many in number,yet too many to win the place with his foot to ſtrike or thruſt home. The ſword & buckler-man can out of his variable,opẽ & gardãt fight, come brauely off & on, falſe and double, ſtrike & thruſt home , & make a true croſſe vpon euery occaſion at his pleaſure:if the Sword & Target mã will flie to his gardãt fight, the bredth of his Target will not ſuffer it , if to his open fight,thẽ hath the Sword & Buckler man in effect the ſword and Buckler to the ſingle , for in that fight by reaſon of the bredth,the target can do litle good or none at all.

The short Staffe.

NOw for the vantage of the ſhort Staffe a-
gainſt the Sword and Buckler , Sword &
26 Target, two hand ſword , ſingle Sword,
Sword and Dagger , or Rapier and Poi-
niard, there is no great queſtion to be made in anie of theſe weapons: whenſoeuer anie blow or thruſt ſhall be ſtrongly made with the ſtaffe, they are euer in falſe place, in the cariage of the wards, for if at any of theſe ſixe weapons he carie his ward high & ſtrōg for his head, as of neceſſitie he muſt carie it verie high, otherwiſe it will be too weake to defend a blow being ſtrongly made at the head , then will his ſpace be too wide, in due time to breake the thruſt from his bodie. Againe, if he carie his ward lower , thereby to be in equall ſpace for readineſſe to breake both blow & thruſt, then in that place his ward is too low, and too weake to defend the blow of the ſtaffe:for the blow being ſtrongly made at the head vpon that ward , will beate downe the ward and his head together, and put him in great danger of his life. And here is to be noted, that if he fight well , the ſtaffe-man neuer ſtriketh but at the head , and thruſteth preſently vnder at the body : and if a blow be firſt made, a thruſt followeth ; & if a thruſt be firſt made, a blow followeth ; and in doing of any of them , the one breedeth the other : ſo that howſoeuer anie of theſe ſixe weapons ſhall carie his ward ſtrongly to defend the firſt, he ſhall be too farre in ſpace to defend the ſecond, whether it be blow or thruſt.

Yet againe for the ſhort ſtaffe : the ſhort ſtaffe hath the vantage againſt the Battel-axe, blacke-bill, or Hal-

bard,

bard: the ſhort ſtaffe hath the vantage,by reaſon of the nimbleneſſe and length: he will ſtrike and thruſt freely, and in better and ſwifter time then can the Battel-axe, Blacke-bill, or Halbard:and by reaſon of his iudgement, diſtance and time,fight ſafe. And this reſolue vpon, the ſhort ſtaffe is the beſt weapon againſt all maner of weapons, the Forreſt bill excepted.

The ſhort ſtaffe or half Pike hath the aduantage againſt two ſword and dagger men, or two Rapiers. Poiniards, and Gantlets.

Alſo the ſhort ſtaffe hath aduantage againſt two Swords and Daggers, or two Rapiers, Poiniards and Gantlets, the reaſons and cauſes before are for the moſt part ſet downe already, the which being well conſidered, you ſhall plainely ſee, that whenſoeuer anie one of the Sword & Dagger men, or Rapier and Poiniard men ſhall breake his diſtance, or ſuffer the Staffe-man to breake his,that man which did firſt breake his diſtãce,or ſuffer the diſtance to be won againſt him, is preſently in danger of death. And this cãnot in reaſon be denied, becauſe the diſtance appertaining to the Staffe-man,either to keepe or breake, ſtandeth vpon the mouing of one large ſpace alwayes at the moſt,both for his offence or ſafety. The other two in the breach of their diſtance to offend the Staffe-man, haue alwayes foure paces at the leaſt therin they fall too great in number with their feet, and too ſhort in diſtance to offend the Staffe-man. Now there reſteth no more to be ſpoken of, but how the Staffe-man ſhall behaue himſelfe to keepe that diſtance, that one of the Sword & Dagger men get not behind him,while the other ſhal buſie him before:to do that is very eaſie,by reaſon of the ſmal nũber of his feet, for by a verie ſmall turning of his feet, as it were in the Center point of a wheele, the other two to keepe their diſtance, are driuen to runne twentie foote for one, as it were vpon the vttermoſt part or circle of the wheele: all this while the Staffe-man is verie well. Then it commeth thus to paſſe, whether they both labour to get behind him, or one keepe directly before him whileſt the other get behind him, yet before that be brought to paſſe, they ſhal either be both before him or iuſt againſt both ſides of him: at which time ſoeuer the Staffe-man finding either of them within diſtance, he preſently in making of his play, ſlayeth with blow or thruſt one of thẽ, or at the leaſt putteth him in great danger of his life. If the Staffe-man take his time, when they are both before him, that is to ſay, before they come to the half ring, iuſt againſt both ſides of the Staffe-man, then he that is neareſt within diſtance is ſlain by blow or thruſt, or put in great danger of his life. But if the Sword and Dagger men do keepe their diſtance vntill they come to the iuſt halfe ring right againſt the ſides of the Staffe-man, and then breake diſtance, that man that firſt breaketh diſtance is ſlaine with blow or thruſt, or ſore hurt, and in great danger of death: and the Staffe-man in making that play at that inſtant, muſt turne with one large pace, the which he may eaſily do, before the other can get neare enough to offend him, by reaſon that he hath to make with his feet but one large pace, but the other hath at the leaſt three paces. But if the Sword and Dagger-men will in the time that they be before him, keep their diſtance in the time of their being vpon the middle part of the outſide of the circle, right againſt both ſides of him, & will labor with all heed & diligence to be both or one of thẽ behind him, that troubleth the Staffe-man nothing at all, for in that very time, when he findeth them paſt the middle part of the circle, he preſently

ſently turneth, by the which he ſhall naturally ſet himſelfe as it were in a triangle, and both the ſword and dagger-men, ſhall thereby ſtand both before him in true diſtance of three paces, from offending of him at the leaſt, as at the firſt they did. And take this for a true ground, there is no man able to ward a ſound blow with the Sword and Dagger, nor Rapier, Poinyard, and Gantlet, being ſtrongly made at the head, with the Staffe, and run in withall, the force of both handes is ſuch, being in his full motion and courſe, that although the other do carie his ward high and ſtrong with both handes, yet his feete being mouing from the ground, the great force of the blow will ſtrike him with his ward, and all downe flat to ground. But if he ſtand faſt with his feete, he may with both weapons together, ſtrongly defend his head from the blow, but then you are ſufficiently inſtructed, the thruſt being preſently made, after the blow full at the bodie, it is impoſſible in due time to breake it, by reaſon of the largeneſſe of his ſpace.

The short Staffe hath the vantage against the long ſtaffe, and Morris Pike, and the Forreſt bill againſt all maner of weapons.

THe reaſons are theſe. The ſhort Staffe 27
hath the vantage of the long Staffe and Morris Pike in his ſtrength & narrownes of ſpace in his foure wardes of defence. And the Forreſt bill hath the vantage of all maner of weapons in his ſtrength and narrownes of ſpace in his eight wardes of defence: and the rather because the Bill hath two wardes for one againſt the Staffe

or Morris Pike, that is to ſay, foure with the Staffe, and foure with the head, and is more offenſiue then is the Staffe or Morris Pike: yet a queſtiõ may be made by the vnskilfull, concerning the fight between the long Staffe and the ſhort, in this ſort: Why ſhould not the long Staffe haue aduantage againſt ſhort Staffe, ſince that the long Staffe-man, being at libertie with his handes, may make his long Staffe both long and ſhort for his beſt aduantage, when he ſhall thinke it good, and therefore when he ſhall find himſelfe ouermatched in the length of his Staffe, by the ſtrength of the ſhort Staffe, and narrowneſſe of ſpace in his foure wardes of defence, he can preſently by drawing backe of his Staffe in his handes, make his Staffe as ſhort as the others, and ſo be readie to fight with him at his owne length. To this I anſwere, that when the long Staffe-man is driuen there to lye, the length of his Staffe that will lye behind him, will hinder him to ſtrike, thruſt, ward, or goe backe in due time. Neither can he turne the contrarie end of his Staffe to keepe out the ſhort Staffe man from the Cloſe, nor ſafely to defend himſelfe at his comming in.

A queſtion.

Anſwere.

Againe of the vantages of weapons.

28 TAke this for a general rule, all long Staues, Morris Pikes, Forreſt bils, Iauelins, or ſuch like long weapons, of what ſort ſoeuer, being aboue the true lengthes, the ſhorteſt haue the aduantage, becauſe they can croſſe and vncroſſe in ſhorter time then can the longer: and all maner of ſhort weapons to be vſed with both handes, as ſtaues, and ſuch like, being vnder the perfect lengthes, the

the longeſt haue the aduantage, and all maner of weapons to be vſed with one hand, that are aboue the perfect length of the ſingle Sword, the ſhorteſt haue the vantage, and all maner of weapons vnder the iuſt length of the ſhort Sword, as Fauchions, Skaines, or Hangers, Woodkniues, Daggers, and ſuch like ſhort weapons of imperfect lengthes, the longeſt haue the aduantage, becauſe the fight of theſe weapons conſiſt within the halfe or quarter Sword, wherein by the ſwift motions of their handes, their eyes are deceiued, and in thoſe weapons, commonly for their handes lieth no defence. And if two ſhall fight with ſtaues or Swordes, or what weapons ſoeuer, the one of them hauing his weapon longer then the perfect length, and the other his weapon ſhorter then the perfect length, he that hath the longeſt hath the vantage, becauſe the ſhorteſt can make no true Croſſe in true time. The ſhort Staffe or halfe Pike, Forreſt bill, Partiſan, or Gleue, or ſuch like weapons of perfect length, to be vſed with both handes, haue the aduantage againſt two Swordes and Daggers, or two Rapiers, Poiniardes, and Gantlets, and againſt all other weapons whatſoeuer, the Forreſt bill excepted.

Againe for the short Staffe or halfe Pike.

THe ſhort Staffe is moſt commonly the 29
beſt weapon of all other, although other weapons may be more offenſiue, and eſpecially againſt manie weapons together, by reaſon of his nimbleneſſe and ſwift motions, and is not much inferiour to the Forreſt bill, although the Forreſt bill be more offenſiue, and hath more wardes, becauſe

the Staffe is verie vncertaine, but the Bill is a more certaine marke, by reason of the breadth of the head, wherby as the Bill hath aduantage in his wardes in the head, so therefore hath the Staffe the like defence, or rather more, to play vpon the head of the Bill, not onely to make a perfect good ward, but thereby, the rather to cast the Bill out of the right line, whereby the Staffe-man may thrust safe, and endanger the Bill-man: and the rather because therein he is the first mouer, wherin there is great vantage, both in time and force. And if the Bilman be not very skilfull (all vantages and disaduantages of both sides considered,) the short Staffe will proue the better weapon. Lastly note this, that long Staues, Morris Pikes, and such like weapons of imperfect lengthes, being to be vsed with both hands, notwithstanding their imperfect lengthes, are perfect weapons to be vsed, the one against the other, and their fightes therein perfect, because in drawing of them backe betwixt their handes, their motions are swifter backewardes, then is the time of the Agents feet forwardes, by the which all their lost times are redeemed: therefore these weapons in their fightes, the one against the other are perfect. And these weapons in the night are the best weapons of all other, and haue great aduantage against the sorrest Bill, short Staffe, or anie maner of short weapons whatsoeuer: for these causes, they boldly make home their fightes, and if neede be against desperate men, that will venture themselues to run in, they redeeme their lost times. But the other with shorter weapons for lacke of light, can make no true defence. Thus endeth the vantages of weapons.

Note this.

Queſtions and anſwers betweene the Scholler and the Maiſter, of the vantages and diſaduantages betweene a tall man, and a man of meane ſtature, hauing both the perfect knowledge in their weapons.

Scholler.

WHo hath the aduantage in fight, of a tall 30
man, or a man of meane ſtature?

Maiſter.

The tall man hath the vantage, for theſe cauſes: his reach being longer, and weapon vnto his ſtature accordingly, he hath thereby a ſhorter courſe with his feet to win the true place, wherin by the ſwift motion of his hand, he may ſtrike or thruſt home: in the which time a man of meane ſtature cannot reach him, & by his large pace, in his true pace in his regreſſion further, ſetteth himſelf out of all danger, & theſe are the vantages that a tall man hath againſt anie man of ſhorter reach then himſelfe.

Tall men haue the vantage againſt men of meane ſtature.

Scholler.

What vantage hath a man of meane ſtature againſt a tall man?

Maiſter.

He hath none: becauſe the true times in fight, and actions accordingly, are to be obſerued and done, as well by a tall man, as by a man of meane ſtature.

Scholler.

Why then if this be true, that tall men haue the vantage againſt mẽ of meane ſtature, it ſhold ſeeme in fight there is no perfection, other then this, when men of like ſtature, reach, & length of weapon, ſhall fight together, the which will ſeldome or neuer happen, but either in the length of their weapons, ſtatures or reaches (if their ſwords ſhould be of iuſt length) ſome difference moſt commonly there will be in their reaches.

Maiſter.

Yes verily, the tall man hath ſtill the vantage, and yet the fight is perfect, although the men that ſhall happen to fight, ſhall happē to be vnequall in their ſtatures, reaches, or lengths of their weapons.

Scholler.

That can I hardly beleeue, vnleſſe you can tell me by Art how to auoid or ſafely defend my ſelfe, being but a man of meane ſtature, againſt a tall man.

Maiſter.

I will tell you: there belongeth vnto this Art of defence onely to be vſed with the feet, progreſſion, regreſſion, trauerſing, and treading of grounds: in any of theſe you playing the part of the Patient, or Patient Agent, your feete are ſwifter in their motions then are the Agents, becauſe his weight and number of his feet in his comming to win the true place to ſtrike or thruſt home, are greater then yours, and therefore the true time is yours to auoid him, or ſafely to defend your ſelfe: ſo the Art is ſtill true, and the tall man hath ſtill the vantage.

Scholler.

Yet I am not fully ſatisfied herein, becauſe you tell me ſtill that the tall man hath the vantage, and notwithſtanding you ſay the Art is true, wherein then hath the tall man the vantage, when by your Art you can defend your ſelfe againſt him.

Maiſter.

Maister.

I will satisfie you therein thus. The tall man hath the vantage, he can maintaine his fight, both by nature and Art, with more ease then can the man of meane stature, because the man of meane stature hath thereby a further course with his feete to passe to the place, wherein he may strike or thrust home, and in winning of that place, is driuen by Art to come garded vnder his wards to defend himselfe, because in the time of his comming, the tall man may both naturally or artificially strike or thrust home, in the which time, if the mā of meane stature should faile in the least iote of his Art, he should be in great daunger of death or hurt. But the tall man can naturally and safely come to the true place open, without any artificiall wards at all, and therein also endanger the other, or driue him still to trauerse his ground, with all the artificiall skill that he hath to defend himselfe; and all this the tall man doth by reason of his length of weapon, large pace, short course, and long reach, with great safetie, pleasure and ease. And for those causes the tall man hath still the vantage of men of meane stature, and yet notwitstāding the noble Science of Defence most perfect and good.

Foure inuincible aduantages consist in a tall man against a man of meane stature. Long reach. Short course. Length of weapō. Large pace.

Of the long single Rapier fight betweene valiant men, hauing both skill, he that is the best wrastler, or if neither of them can wrastle, the strongest man most commonly killeth the other, or leaueth him at his mercie.

WHen two valiant men of skill at single Rapier do fight, one or both of them most cōmonly standing vpon their strength or skill in wrastling, will presently seeke to run into 31 the cloſe; but hauing both skill, not without ſpeciall care of their gard or croſſe, the which they may ſafely do, by reaſon of the length of their Rapiers: but hapning both of one mind, the rather do bring themſelues together: that being done, noskil with Rapiers auaileth, they preſently grapple faſt their hilts, wriſts, armes, bodies or neckes, as in luſtring, wraſtling, or ſtriuing together, they may beſt find for their aduantages: wherby it moſt commonly falleth out, that he that is the beſt wraſtler, or ſtrongeſt man (if neither of them can wraſtle) ouercommeth, wreſting by ſtrength, or fine skill in wraſtling, the Rapier from his aduerſarie, or caſting him frō him, either to the ground, or to ſuch diſtance, that he may by reaſon therof, vſe the edge or point of his rapier, to ſtrike or thruſt him, leauing him dead or aliue at his mercie. But if but one of theſe valiant men ſhall ſeeke to run into the cloſe, and that the other ſhall vſe his skill in trauerſing of his ground, or otherwiſe by ſtanding vpon his gard or *Stocata* ward, to take all maner of aduātages at his cōming, yet all auaileth him not, becauſe the Rapiers being long, the croſſing of the blades cannot be auoided: that being made, the oppreſſor runneth faſter forwards then can the defendant backwards, and ſo are brought together, as in the firſt aſſault they were, & euerie action therein accordingly performed.

Of the Rapier and Poiniard-fight betwixt valiant men, hauing both skill.

32 IF two valiant men do fight at Rapier and Poiniard hauing both skill, one or both of them will preſently preſſe hard to winne the place, wherein in his iudgement he may thruſt home. If both

be

be of one mind, the time is doubled in winning the ſame: whereby it commeth to paſſe, that then he that firſt thruſteth, endangereth, killeth or hurteth the other: and if they both thruſt together, as they may do by the equall time of their feet, then they are moſt commonly both ſlaine, or both hurt. And this is well knowne vnto all men of skill, that the place being once gotten, there is neither iudgement, ſpace, pace, nor time, either by wards with their Rapier blades, or by breaking with their Poiniards, or flying backe, that can preſerue or defend them. But if but one of them will ſeeke to win by paſſage, hard preſſing, or otherwiſe the place, wherin in his iudgement he may thruſt home, it is impoſſible for the other to denie him the ſame, becauſe the length of the Rapiers winneth him the croſſe; the croſſe being taken, the place is had; the place being had, he that firſt thruſteth, firſt ſpeedeth: if both thruſt together, they are both in danger: thē preſently followeth (vnleſſe it pleaſe God otherwiſe to haue it) the ſtabs with their daggers, wherein there lieth no defence.

Of the long Rapier & Poiniard-fight betweene two valiant men, the one hauing skil, the other none: that he that hath no skill hath the vantage.

WHen two valiant men ſhal fight with lōg 33
Rapiers and Poiniards, the one hauing skill, and the other none, he that hath no skill moſt commōly proueth himſelf the better mā, for theſe cauſes or reaſons following. Firſt the skilfull man as knowing the other to haue no skill, or finding it to be ſo by his ſhape or

maner of comming towardes him, will presently yeeld to take the aduantage of his comming, or else with all speed put himselfe into his short ward, to be readie at his comming to make out a strong *Stocata* (as the *Italians* call it:) the other knowing his imperfection in fight, assureth himselfe there can be no great good for him to stand long out at the point, presently redoubleth or reuiueth his spirits with perfect resolution, to make short worke, couragiously with some offensiue action, such as nature shall best yeeld vnto him, flieth in with all force and agilitie: the skilfull man standeth watching to take such aduantages as his schoolemaister hath taught him, in the which time, manie times it falleth out, he is taught a new time, euen by an vnskilfull man that neuer fought before, is sore hurt or slaine: and if it happen they both misse in their offensiue actions, then by reason thereof, and of the imperfect length of their Rapiers, they come to stabbing with their Poiniards, wherin there lyeth no defence, because distance being broken, iudgement faileth, time is lost, and their eies (by the swift motions of their handes) are deceiued.

Of the long single Rapier, or Rapier and Poiniard-fight betweene two vnskilfull men being valiant.

34 WHen two vnskilfull men (being valiant) shall fight with long single Rapiers, there is lesse danger in that kind of fight, by reason of their distance in conuenient length, waight, and vnweildinesse, then is with short Rapiers: whereby it commeth to passe, that what hurt shall happen to be done, if anie with the edge or point of their Rapiers

Rapiers is done in a moment, and preſently will grapple and wraſtle together, wherin moſt commonly the ſtrongeſt or beſt Wraſtler ouercommeth, and the like fight falleth out betweene them, at the long Rapier and Poiniard, but much more deadly, becauſe in ſtead of Cloſe and Wraſtling, they fall moſt commonly to ſtabbing with their Poiniardes.

Of the imperfection and inſufficiencie of Rapiers in generall, of what length ſoeuer they be.

35

If they ſtand vpon breaking with their Daggers, he that firſt winneth the place, and thruſteth home, hurteth the other for lacke of the circūference: if both thruſt together, they are both ſped, becauſe their Spaces of Defence are too wide to anſwere the time of the hand, and by the ſwift motion thereof, the eye in that diſtance is by the ſame deceiued.

The feete in their courſe, but not in the firſt motion, alwaies note for the auoiding of great errours.

IF two fight with long Rapiers, vpon euerie Croſſe made within the halfe Rapier, if they haue Poiniardes, they moſt commonly ſtabbe each other, which cannot be auoided, because the Rapiers being long, the Croſſe cannot be vndone of either ſide, without going backe with their feete, the which likewiſe in due time cannot be done, becauſe the hand is more ſwifter then the feete, and the feete more ſwifter in their courſe forwardes then backwardes, neither can the Croſſe be preuented, becauſe the point of neceſſitie lyeth too farre off in his offence, or elſe within compaſſe of the true time of the hand and bodie, by reaſon of his imperfect length: and ſo by the like reaſons, if two fight with long ſingle Rapiers, vpon euerie Croſſe made therewith, within the halfe Rapier, the Cloſe cannot be auoided, wherby it commeth to paſſe moſt commonly, that the ſtrongeſt man or beſt Wraſtler ouercommeth. Now if two do fight with ſhort Rapiers, or Rapiers of conuenient length, ſuch Rapiers be inconuenient and inſufficient alſo for lacke of an hilt to defend the hand and head from the blow; for no eie (in making a perfect ward for the head, to defend a blow, can discerne to take the same within three or foure inches, wherby it may as well and as often fall vpon the hand, as vpon the blade of the Rapier. Againe, the hilt as well serueth to defend the head as the hand, and is a more sure and strong ward, then is the blade of the Rapier. And further, vnderstand this for truth, that in gardant and open fight, the hand without an hilt lieth open to most blowes that shalbe stroken by the Agent, out of the gardant or open fight, because in the true cariage of the gardant fight, the hand must lie aboue the head, in such straightnes and narrownes of space, that which way soeuer the Agent shall strike or thrust at the head, face, or bodie, the remouing of two or foure inches shall saue all. And now somewhat more for the shortnesse or conuenient length of Rapiers.

Rapiers hauing no hilts to defend the head, the Rapier-man is driuen of necessitie to lie at the variable fight or low ward, and being there he can neither defend in due time, head, face, nor bodie from the blowes or thrustes of him, that shall fight out of the gardant or open fight, but is continually in great danger of the Agent, for these causes following. First, because his space is too wide to defend his head from blow or thrust. Secondly his Pace standing vpon that fight, wilbe of necessitie too great or too narrow: if too narrow, too weak: if too large, his weight and number of his feet, are too great to endanger him, that is vpon his gardant or open fight.

Of

Of the imperfection and inſufficiencie of the ſight of the ſingle Rapier, Rapier and Poiniard, Rapier and Buckler, Rapier and Cloke, and Rapier and Gloue of maile.

THe Rapier fight, whether it be ſingle or accōpanied with Poiniard, Buckler, cloke, or gloue of male, is ſtill by reaſon of the inſufficiencie or imperfection of the Rapier, an imperfect fight: vnperfect inſtruments can make no perfect muſicke, neither can vnperfect weapons make perfect fight: let the men that handle them haue all the knowledge that may be in all maner of weapons, yea the full height, or perfection, and true habite by his great labour and induſtry, euen as it were naturally effected in him, yet if the weapons that they ſhall fight withall be imperfect or inſufficient to performe whatſoeuer appertaineth vnto true fight, as concerning the perfection of their ſafetie, it auaileth them nothing. What ſhall we then ſay for the Rapier? Is the Rapier an imperfect or inſufficient weapon to perfourme whatſoeuer appertaineth vnto the true fight? Yea: Wherefore? Becauſe vnto the true fight there appertaineth foure fights, Gardant fight, Open fight, Variable fight, and Cloſe fight: without all foure of theſe fights it is impoſſible to fight ſafe: but the Rapier for lacke of an hilt is an vnperfect weapon, and therefore inſufficient to fight ſafe vpon theſe foure fights, the reaſons are alreadie ſet downe in the Paradoxe before, but it is inferred to looſe the benefit of two of the 36 beſt fights, gardant and open fight,and to flie from thē, and truſt only vnto variable fight, and cloſe fight. Now hauing proued through the imperfection or inſufficiencie of the Rapier, the imperfection of the Rapier fight, it remaineth that I ſpeake of the reſt of the weapons, or inſtruments appertaining vnto Rapier fight.

The Rapier and Poiniard fight, the Rapier & Buckler fight, the Rapier and cloke fight,& the Rapier & gloue of male fight: all theſe fights by reaſon of the imperfection of the Rapier, and Rapier fight, are all alſo imperfect fights: and for proofe of the vncertaintie and impoſſibilities of ſafetie in any of theſe fights, thus it ſtandeth. Theſe fights depend altogether vpō variable fight and cloſe fight: in anie of theſe fights it is impoſſible in true ſpace of Offence to keepe the blades of their Rapiers from croſſing, or frō breaking with the Poiniards, buckler, cloke, or breaking or catching with the gloue of male; becauſe in anie of theſe two fights, the Agent hath ſtill in true ſpace the blade of the Patients Rapier to worke vpon. Theſe things by letters cannot be made more plaine, neither is it vnknowne to the skilfull, or in fight by anie meanes to be auoided, the weapon being too farre in true ſpace to be wrought vpon, the place cannot be denied, do the patient Agent what he can for his life to the contrarie,either by blowes,thruſts, falſing,or doubling of thruſts,going backe, indirections, or turnings of the body, or what elſe ſoeuer may in the higheſt touch of wit or ſtrength, or agilitie of bodie be deuiſed or done,to keepe out the Agent: but ſtill the Agent by narrowneſſe of ſpace bringeth himſelf by ſtrōg gard to the place, where being brought,it is as impoſſible to fight ſafe, as it is for two deſperate men ſet together

ther

ther being both blind;becauſe in the true place (wonne in Rapier or variable fight) their eyes by the ſwift motions of their hands are deceiued , the croſſes in that fight are falſe, their diſtance, iudgements and times are loſt,either to offend in ſafetie, or ſafely to defend themſelues : and theſe reaſons, rules, or grounds of the feates of armes are infallible and inuincible.

Now, ô you Italian teachers of Defence , where are your *Stocatas*, *Imbrocatas* ,*Mandritas* ,*Puntas*, & *Puynta reuerſas*,*Stramiſons* ,*Paſſatas*,*Carricados*,*Amazzas*, &*Incartatas*,& playing with your bodies , remouing with your feet a litle aſide,circle wiſe winding of your bodies, making of three times with your feet together,marking with one eye the motion of the aduerſary,&with the other eye the aduātage of thruſting? What is become of all theſe iugling gambalds , Apiſh deuiſes,with all the reſt of your ſquint-eyed trickes , when as through your deepe ſtudies, long practiſes, & apt bodies, both ſtrong & agilious, you haue attained to the height of all theſe things? What then auaileth it you, when you ſhal come to fight for your liues with a man of skill?you ſhall haue neither time,nor place,in due time to performe any one of them , nor gardant nor open fight ſafely to keep out a man of skill,a man of no skill, or ſcholler of your owne teaching, from the true place, the place of ſafetie , the place of vncertaintie or miſchiefe , the place of wounds or death,but are there inforced to ſtand in that miſchieuous, vncertaine, dangerous, and moſt deadly place, as two men hauing loſt in part their chiefeſt ſences, moſt furiouſly with their rapiers or poiniards , wounding or ſlaying each other.

Thus endeth the imperfect fights of the rapier with

all maner of weapons or instruments thereto ap pertaining, with their imperfections, through the true groũds and rules of the Art of armes, truly displayed & brought to light.

All laud be vnto the Almighty God.

That the reasons vsed by the Italian Fencers in commending the vse of the Rapier and Poiniard, because it maketh peace, maketh against themselues.

37 IT hath bin commonly held, that since the Italians haue taught the Rapier fight, by reason of the dangerous vse therof, it hath bred great ciuilitie amongst our English nation, they will not now giue the lye, nor with such foule speeches abuse themselues, therefore there are fewer frayes in these times then were wont to be: it cannot be denied but this is true, that we are more circumspect of our words, and more fearefull to fight, then heretofore we haue bene. But whereof commeth it? Is it from this, that the Rapier maketh peace in our minds; or from hence, that it is not so sufficient defence for our bodies in our fight? He that will fight when he is armed, will not fight when he is naked: is it therefore good to go naked to keepe peace? he that would fight with his Sword and Buckler, or Sword and Dagger, being weapons of true defence, will not fight with his Rapier and Poiniard, wherein no true defence or fight is perfect: are these insufficiẽt weapõs therfore the better, because not being sufficiẽt to defẽd vs in fight, they force vs vnto peace? What else is it, but to say, it is good for

There are few frayes, but more valiant Gentlemẽ slaine now then were then.

subiects

ſubiects to be poore, that they may not go to law: or to lacke munition, that they may not fight, nor go to the warres: and to conclude, what more followeth through the imperfect workes of theſe *Italian* peacemakers? They haue made many a ſtrong man in his fight weake, many a valiant man fearefull, manie a worthie man truſting to their imperfect fight, hath bene ſlaine, and manie of our deſperate boyes and young youthes, to become in that Rapier-fight, as good men as *England* yeeldeth, and the talleſt men in this land, in that fight as verie boyes as they and no better. This good haue the *Italian* teachers of Offence done vs, they haue transformed our boyes into men, and our men into boyes, our ſtrong men into weakeneſſe, our valiant men doubtfull, and manie worthie men reſoluing themſelues vpon their falſe reſolutions, haue moſt wilfully in the field, with their Rapiers ended their liues. And laſtly, haue left to remaine amongſt vs after their deathes, theſe inconueniences behind them, falſe Fence-bookes, imperfect weapons, falſe fightes, and euill cuſtomes, whereby for lacke of vſe and practiſe in perfect weapons and true fight, we are diſabled for the ſeruice of our Prince, defence of our countrey, and ſafetie of our liues in priuate fight.

That the ſhort Sword hath the aduantage againſt the long Sword or long Rapier.

WHereas for the moſt part opinions are 38
generally holden, that the long Sword, or long Rapier, hath the vantage in fight againſt the ſhort Sword, which the *Italian* teachers of Defence, by their falſe de-

monſtratiōs haue brought vs to beleeue. I haue thought good that the truth may appeare which hath the vantage, to adde my helpe vnto the reaſons they vſe in their owne behalfe, for that yet I could neuer heare them make a ſound reaſon for the ſame. Theſe are the reaſons. First with my long Rapier, I will put my ſelfe into my gard or *Stocata*, holding my hilt backe by the outſide of my right thigh, keeping in ſhort the point of my Rapier, ſo as he that hath the ſhort Sword, ſhall not be able to reach the point of my Rapier, to make his ward or Croſſe with his Dagger, Buckler, Sword, or Cloke, without ſtepping in of his foote, the which time is too long to anſwere the time of the hand, by reaſon of my diſtance. I can there ſtand ſafe without danger of blow or thruſt, playing the Patients part: if you ſtrike or thruſt you do it too ſhort, by reaſon of my diſtance: if you ſeek to come nearer, you muſt do it with the time of your foote, in the which time I may ſafely thruſt home: if in that diſtance you breake it not, you are ſlaine: if you do breake it, yet you do me no harme, by reaſon of my diſtance, and I may ſtand faſt and thruſt againe, or flie backe at my pleaſure: ſo haue you put your ſelfe in danger of your life, and hauing hardly eſcaped, are driuen againe to begin a new bought, as at the firſt you did. Againe, if I pleaſe, I can be the oppreſſour, keeping the ſame gard, and my point in ſhort as I did before, and preſſing ſtrongly by putting in by litle and litle of my feete, vntill the place with my foote be gotten, wherein (in my iudgement) I may thruſt home, the which I may boldly and ſafely do, without reſpect of anie ward at all, by reaſon of my diſtance, in which time of my comming he muſt ſtrike, thruſt, ward, or go backe: if he go backe, it

Theſe reaſons are vſed by the Italians.

it is a great diſgrace: if he ſtrike or thruſt, it is too ſhort: if he ſtand to defend, the place being alreadie gotten, where I may thruſt home, the thruſt being verie quicke & ſtrongly made, ſuch is the force and ſwiftneſſe thereof, that it is impoſſible by nature or art, for anie man to breake one thruſt of an hundred. Theſe reaſons in my opinion may ſuffice to confirme the wiſe, that there is no queſtion to be made, but that the long Rapier hath the aduantage againſt the ſhort Sword.

A confutation of the Italians reaſons.

Sir you haue pretily handled your diſcourſe, concerning the vantages of the long Rapier againſt the ſhort Sword, eſpecially at the firſt ſhew, and according to common ſence, but for the ſubſtance and truth of the true fight, you haue ſaid nothing, becauſe for the performance of anie of your allegations, you haue neither true Pace, Place, Time, nor Space: theſe are the reaſons. Your Pace of neceſſitie muſt be too large, becauſe otherwiſe you cannot keepe ſafe the point of your long Rapier, from the Croſſe of the ſhort Sword, vnleſſe you will with a narrow Pace keepe backe your hilt ſo farre, that the ſpace of your offence wilbe too large or too long in diſtance, and your bodie vnapt to moue and to thruſt both ſtrong and quicke in due time, nor aptly to keepe your diſtance, to win the place with your feete, to thruſt home. So now you may plainely ſee, if you haue skill in the art or ſcience of Defence, that to performe anie thing which you haue alleadged, you haue neither true Pace, Place, time nor Space. But if you will ſtand vpon the largeneſſe of your Pace, to keepe backe or ſaue the point of your long Rapier from the ward or Croſſe of the ſhort Sword, or vpon your *Paſſatos*, in all theſe you haue great diſaduantages: and these are my reasons: Your number will be too great, as thus: whensoeuer you meane out of your large pace to thrust home, you must of necessitie make foure times with your feet, and one with your hand, or two times with your feet, and one with your hand at the least: and whensoeuer you make any of your passages, the nūber of your feet are greater then the greatest of any of these times done out of the large pace: but the patient with his short sword, to auoyd you, or disappoint you of your thrust, hath but one time with his foot, at or before the which time, as he in his iudgemēt shall find you in your motion, hath by the slow and great number of your motions or times, sufficient time safely out of all danger to make himselfe readie to take his crosse with his short sword. Now Sir, whether you thrust or not thrust, whether you play the part of an Agent, or Patient, it helpeth you nothing, for he that hath the short sword hath foure times or motions against the long Rapier, namely, bent, spent, lying spent, and drawing backe, in all maner of fights these are to be obserued both by the Patient and Agent. Now note, he that hath the long Rapier must of necessitie play vpon one of these foure motions, or be Patient, which soeuer he shall do, he is still in great danger of the crosse of the short sword, because if he be Agent, his number is too great, he falleth into one of the foure motions, the Patient with his short sword, hauing but the time of the hand, or hād & foot, safely vpon these actions or times taketh his crosse with the short Sword: that being done, he presently vncrosseth and striketh or thrusteth at his pleasure him that hath the long Rapier, in the head, face, or bodie. Now here is againe to be noted, that when the crosse is made, if he that hath the long Rapier ſtand faſt, he is wounded preſently in the vncroſſing of the ſhort ſword, if he ſtep or leape backe to ſaue himſelfe, yet the time of the hand being ſwifter then the time of the foot, ouertaketh him, with blow or thruſt in the arme, hand, head, face and bodie. Now if he that hath the long Rapier will be patient & make no play, but lie ſtill watching to make his thruſt or *Stocata* iuſt in the comming or mouing of the Agents feete with his ſhort ſword, then he hath as great diſaduantage as he had when he was Patient, becauſe thē the Agent with his ſhort Sword hath but hand and foot to make his croſſe: which is moſt ſafely to be done in that time, which we call Bent, and is as impoſſible for the Rapier-man to preuent, as it is for an vnskilfull to ſtrike or thruſt iuſt together with a man of skill. Then thus I conclude, that he that fighteth with a long Rapier, againſt him that fighteth with a ſhort Sword, can do nothing in due time to defend himſelfe, or hurt the other, but is ſtill in daunger of his life, or at the mercie of him that hath the ſhort Sword, or elſe hath no ſafe way to helpe himſelfe, but onely *Cobs* Trauerſe. This *Cob* was a great quareller, and did delight in great brauerie to giue foule words to his betters, and would not refuſe to go into the field to fight with any man, and when he came into the field, would draw his Sword to fight, for he was ſure by the cunning of his Trauerſe, not to be hurt by anie man: for at anie time finding himſelfe ouermatched would ſuddenly turne his backe and runne away with ſuch ſwiftneſſe, that it was thought a good horſe would ſcarce take him. And this when I was a young man, was verie much ſpoken of by many Gentlemen of the Innes of

Cobs Trauerſe.

the Court, and was called *Cobs* Trauerſe and thoſe that had ſeene anie go backe too faſt in his fight, would ſay, he did tread *Cobs* Trauerſe.

George Siluer his militarie riddle, truly ſet downe betweene the Perfection and Imperfection of fight: containing the handling of the foure fights: wherein true conſiſteth the whole ſumme and full perfection of the true fight, with all maner of weapons, with an inuicible concluſion.

GArdant fight ſtayeth, putteth backe, or beateth gardant fight.

Open fight ſtayeth, putteth backe, or beateth open fight.

Variable fight anſwereth variable fight in the firſt diſtance, and not otherwiſe, except it be with the perfect length againſt the imperfect.

Cloſe fight is beaten by gardant fight.

Variable cloſe & gardant fight, beateth gardant fight, open fight, variable fight, and cloſe fight.

Gardant fight in the imperfection of the Agent or Patient, winneth the halfe ſword, and preuenteth the cloſe, and whoſoeuer firſt ventureth the cloſe, looſeth it, and is in great danger of death, and not poſſible to eſcape or get out againe without great hurt.

There attendeth moſt diligently vpon theſe foure fights foure offenſiue actions, which we call certaine, vncertaine, firſt, before, iuſt, and afterwards: they are to be performed through iudgement, time, meaſure, number and waight, by which all maner of blowes, thruſts,

thruſts, falſes, doubles, or ſlips, are preuented, or moſt ſafely defended. And thus endeth my riddle.

Now followeth the concluſion, that whoſoeuer ſhall thinke or find himſelfe in his fight too weake for the Agent, or Patient Agent, and therefore, or by reaſon of his drunkenneſſe, or vnreaſonable deſperateneſſe ſhall preſe within the halfe Sword, or deſeratel runne in of purpoſe to giue hurt, or at leaſt for taking of one hurt, to giue another, ſhall moſt aſſuredly be in great daunger of death or wounds, and the other ſhall ſtill be ſafe and go free.

Veritas vincit.

A BRIEFE NOTE OF THREE ITA-*lian Teachers of Offence.*

I write not this to diſgrace the dead, but to ſhew their impudēt boldneſſe and inſufficiency in performance of their profeſſion when they were liuing: that from henceforth this briefe note may be a remembrance and warning to beware of bad I wiſt.

THere were three Italian Teachers of Offence in my time. The firſt was *Signior Rocko*: the ſecond was *Ieronimo*, that was *Signior Rocko* his boy, that taught Gentlemen in the *Blacke-Fryers*, as Vſher for his maiſter in ſteed of a man. The third was *Vincentio*. This *Signior Rocko* came into *England* about ſome thirtie yeares paſt: he taught the Noblemen & Gentlemen of the Court; he cauſed ſome of them to weare leaden ſoales in their ſhoes, the better to bring them to nimbleneſſe of feet in their fight. He disburſed a great ſumme of mony for the leaſe of a faire houſe in *Warwicke* lane, which he called his Colledge, for he thought it great diſgrace for him to keepe a Fence-ſchoole, he being then thought to be the onely famous Maiſter of the Art of armes in the whole world. He cauſed to be fairely drawne and ſet round about his Schoole all the Noblemens and Gentlemens armes that were his Schollers, and hanging right vnder their armes their Rapiers, daggers, gloues of male and gantlets. Alſo, he had benches and ſtooles, the roome being verie large, for Gentlemē to ſit round about his Schoole to behold his teaching. He taught none commonly vnder twentie, fortie, fifty, or an hundred pounds. And becauſe all things ſhould be verie neceſſary for the Noblemē & gentlemē, he had

in

in his ſchoole a large ſquare table, with a greene carpet, done round with a verie brode rich fringe of gold, alwaies ſtanding vpon it a verie faire Standiſh couered with Crimſon Veluet, with inke, pens, pin-duſt, and ſealing waxe, and quiers of verie excellent fine paper gilded, readie for the Noblemen & Gentlemen (vpon occaſion) to write their letters, being then deſirous to follow their fight, to ſend their men to diſpatch their buſineſſe. And to know how the time paſſed, he had in one corner of his ſchoole a Clocke, with a verie faire large Diall, he had within that ſchoole, a roome the which was called his priuie ſchoole, with manie weapons therein, where he did teach his ſchollers his ſecret fight, after he had perfectly taught them their rules. He was verie much beloued in the Court.

There was one *Auſten Bagger*, a verie tall gentleman of his handes, not ſtanding much vpon his skill, but carying the valiant hart of an Fngliſhman, vpon a time being merrie amongſt his friendes, ſaid he would go fight with *Signior Rocco*, preſently went to *Signior Rocco* his houſe in the *Blackefriers*, and called to him in this maner: *Signior Rocco*, thou that art thought to be the onely cunning man in the world with thy weapon, thou that takeſt vpon thee to hit anie Engliſhman with a thruſt vpon anie button, thou that takeſt vpon thee to come ouer the ſeas, to teach the valiant Noblemen and Gentlemen of *England* to fight, thou cowardly fellow come out of thy houſe if thou dare for thy life, I am come to fight with thee. *Signior Rocco* looking out at a window, perceiuing him in the ſtreet to ſtand readie with his Sword and Buckler, with his two hand Sword drawne, with all ſpeed ran into the ſtreet, and manfully let flie at *Austen Bagger*, who most brauely defended himselfe, and presently closed with him, and stroke vp his heeles, and cut him ouer the breech, and trode vpon him, and most grieuously hurt him vnder his feet: yet in the end *Austen* of his good nature gaue him his life, and there left hin. This was the first and last fight that euer *Signior Rocco* made, sauing once at Queene Hith he drew his Rapier vpon a waterman, where he was throughly beaten with Oares and Stretchers, but the oddes of their weapons were as great against his Rapier, as was his two hand Sword against *Austen Baggers* Sword and Buckler, therefore for that fray he was to be excused.

Then came in *Vincentio* and *Ieronimo*, they taught Rapier-fight at the Court, at *London*, and in the countrey, by the space of seauen or eight yeares or thereabouts.These two *Italian* Fencers, especially *Vincentio*, said that Englishmen were strong men, but had no cunning, and they would go backe too much in their fight, which was great disgrace vnto them.Vpon these words of disgrace against Englishmen, my brother *Toby Siluer* and my selfe, made challenge against them both, to play with them at the single Rapier, Rapier and Dagger, the single Dagger, the single Sword, the Sword and Target, the Sword and Buckler, & two hand Sword, the Staffe, battell Axe, and Morris Pike, to be played at the Bell Saua ge vpon the Scaffold, where he that went in his fight faster backe then he ought, of Englishman or Italian, shold be in danger to breake his necke off the Scaffold. We caused to that effect, fiue or sixe score Bils of challenge to be printed, and set vp from *Southwarke* to the Tower, and from thence through *London* vnto *Westminster*,

minster, we were at the place with all these weapons at the time apointed, within a bow shot of their Fence schoole: many gentlemen of good accompt, caried manie of the bils of chalenge vnto them, telling them that now the *Siluers* were at the place appointed, with all their weapons, looking for them, and a multitude of people there to behold the fight, saying vnto them, now come and go with vs (you shall take no wrong) or else you are shamed for euer. Do the gentlemen what they could, these gallants would not come to the place of triall. I verily thinke their cowardly feare to answere this chalenge, had vtterly shamed them indeed, had not the maisters of Defence of *London*, within two or three daies after, bene drinking of bottell Ale hard by *Vincentios* schoole, in a Hall where the *Italians* must of necessitie passe through to go to their schoole: and as they were comming by, the maisters of Defence did pray them to drinke with them, but the *Italians* being verie cowardly, were afraide, and presently drew their Rapiers: there was a pretie wench standing by, that loued the *Italians*, she ran with ourcrie into the street, helpe, helpe, the *Italians* are like to be slaine: the people with all speede came running into the house, and with their Cappes and such things as they could get, parted the fraie, for the English maisters of Defence, meant nothing lesse then to foile their handes vpon these two faint-harted fellowes. The next morning after, all the Court was filled, that the *Italian* teachers of Fence had beaten all the maisters of Defence in *London*, who set vpon them in a house together. This wan the *Italian* Fencers their credit againe, and thereby got much, still continuing their false teaching to the end of their liues.

This *Vincentio* proued himſelfe a ſtout man not long before he died, that it might be ſeene in his life time he had bene a gallant, and therefore no maruaile he tooke vpon him ſo highly to teach Engliſhmen to fight, and to ſet forth bookes of the feates of Armes. Vpon a time at *Wels* in Somerſetſhire, as he was in great brauerie amongſt manie gentlemen of good accompt, with great boldneſſe he gaue out ſpeeches, that he had bene thus manie yeares in *England*, and ſince the time of his firſt comming, there was not yet one Engliſhman, that could once touch him at the ſingle Rapier, or Rapier and Dagger. A valiant gentleman being there amongſt the reſt, his Engliſh hart did riſe to heare this proude boaſter, ſecretly ſent a meſſenger to one *Bartholomew Bramble* a friend of his, a verie tall man both of his hands and perſon, who kept a ſchoole of Defence in the towne, the meſſenger by the way made the maiſter of Defence acquainted with the mind of the gentleman that ſent for him, and of all what *Vincentio* had ſaid, this maiſter of Defence preſently came, and amongſt all the gentlemen with his cap off, prayed maiſter *Vincentio*, that he would be pleaſed to take a quart of wine of him. *Vincentio* verie ſcornefully looking vpon him, ſaid vnto him. Wherefore ſhould you giue me a quart of wine? Marie Sir, ſaid he, becauſe I heare you are a famous man at your weapon. Then preſently ſaid the gentleman that ſent for the maiſter of Defence: Maiſter *Vincentio*, I pray you bid him welcome, he is a man of your profeſſion. My profeſſion ſaid *Vincentio*? what is my profeſſion. Then ſaid the gentleman, he is a maiſter of the noble ſcience of Defence. Why ſaid maiſter *Vincttio*, God make him a good man. But the maiſter of Defençe wold

not

not thus leaue him, but prayed him againe he would be pleased to take a quart of wine of him. Thē said *Vincētio*, I haue no need of thy wine. Then said the maister of Defence: Sir I haue a schoole of Defence in the towne, will it please you to go thither. Thy schoole, said maister *Vincentio*? what shall I do at thy schoole? play with me (said the maister) at the Rapier and Dagger, if it please you. Play with thee said maister *Vincentio*? if I play with thee, I will hit thee 1. 2. 3. 4. thrustes in the eie together. Then said the maister of Defence, if you can do so, it is the better for you, and the worse for me, but surely I can hardly beleeue that you can hit me: but yet once againe I hartily pray you good Sir, that you will go to my schoole, and play with me. Play with thee said maister *Vincentio* (verie scornefully?) by God me scorne to play with thee. With that word scorne, the maister of Defence was verie much moued, and vp with his great English fist, and stroke maister *Vincentio* such a boxe on the eare that he fell ouer and ouer, his legges iust against a Butterie hatch, whereon stood a great blacke Iacke: the maister of Defence fearing the worst, against *Vincentio* his rising, catcht the blacke Iacke into his hand, being more then halfe full of Beere. *Vincentio* lustily start vp, laying his hand vpon his Dagger, & with the other hand pointed with his finger, saying, very well: I will cause to lie in the Gaile for this geare, 1. 2. 3 4. yeares. And well said the maister of Defence, since you will drinke no wine, will you pledge me in Beere? I drinke to all the cowardly knaues in *England*, and I thinke thee to be the veriest coward of them all: with that he cast all the Beere vpon him: notwithstanding *Vincentio* hauing nothing but his guilt Rapier, and

Dagger about him, and the other for his defence the blacke Iacke, would not at that time fight it out: but the next day met with the maister of Defence in the streete, and said vnto him, you remember how misused a me yesterday, you were to blame, me be an excellent man, me teach you how to thrust two foote further then anie Englishman, but first come you with me: then he brought him to a Mercers shop, and said to the Mercer, let me see of your best silken Pointes, the Mercer did presently shew him some of seauen groates a dozen, then he payeth fourteene groates for two dozen, and said to the maister of Defence, there is one dozen for you, and here is another for me. This was one of the valiantest Fencers that came from beyond the seas, to teach Englishmen to fight, and this was one of the manliest frayes, that I haue hard of, that euer he made in *England*, wherin he shewed himselfe a farre better man in his life, then in his profession he was, for he professed armes, but in his life a better Christian. He set forth in print a booke for the vse of the Rapier and Dagger, the which he called his practise, I haue read it ouer ,and because I finde therein neither true rule for the perfect teaching of true fight, not true ground of true fight, neither sence or reason for due proofe thereof. I haue thought it friuolous to recite any part therin contained: yet that the truth hereof may appeare, let two mẽ being wel experienced in the Rapier and Dagger fight, choose any of the best branches in the same booke, & make trial with force and agility, without the which the truth betweene the true & false fight cannot be knowne, & they shall find great imperfections therein. And againe, for proofe that there is no truth, neither in his rules, groũds

or

or Rapier-fight, let triall be made in this maner: Set two vnskilfull men together at the Rapier and Dagger, being valiant, and you ſhall ſee, that once in two boutes there ſhall either one or both of them be hurt. Then ſet two skilfull men together, being valiant at the Rapier and Dagger, and they ſhall do the like. Then ſet a skilful Rapier and Dagger-man the beſt that can be had, and a valiant man hauing no skill together at Rapier & Dagger, and once in two bouts vpon my credit in all the experience I haue in fight, the vnskilful man, do the other what he can for his life to the contrarie, ſhall hurt him, and moſt commonly if it were in continuance of fight, you ſhall ſee the vnskilfull man to haue the aduantage. And if I ſhould chuſe a valiant man for ſeruice of the Prince, or to take part with me or anie friend of mine in a good quarrell, I would chuſe the vnskilfull man, being vnencombred with falſe fights, becauſe ſuch a man ſtandeth free in his valour with ſtrength and agilitie of bodie, freely taketh the benefit of nature, fighteth moſt braue, by looſing no oportunitie, either ſoundly to hurt his enemie, or defend himſelfe, but the other ſtanding for his Defence, vpon his cunning Italian wardes, *Pointa reuerſa*, the *Imbrocata*, *Stocata*, and being faſt tyed vnto theſe falſe fightes, ſtandeth troubled in his wits, and nature therby racked through the largeneſſe or falſe lyings or Spaces, whereby he is in his fight as a man halfe maimed, looſing the oportunity of times & benefit of nature, & whereas before being ignorant of theſe falſe Rapier fightes, ſtanding in the free libertie of nature giuen him by god, he was able in the field with his weapō to anſwere the valianteſt man in the world, but now being tied vnto that falſe fickle vncertaine fight, there-

Proofes againſt the Rapier fight.

by hath loſt in nature his freedome, is now become ſcarce halfe a man, and euerie boye in that fight is become as good a man as himſelfe.

Ieronimo this gallant was valiant, and would fight indeed, and did, as you ſhall heare. He being in a Coch with a wench that he loued well, there was one *Cheeſe*, a verie tall man, in his fight naturall Engliſh, for he fought with his Sword and Dagger, and in Rapier-fight had no skill at all. This *Cheeſe* hauing a quarrell to *Ieronimo*, ouertooke him vpon the way, himſelfe being on horſebacke, did call to *Ieronimo*, and bad him come forth of the Coch or he would fetch him, for he was come to fight with him. *Ieronimo* preſently went forth of the Coch and drew his Rapier and dagger, put himſelf into his beſt ward or *Stocata*, which ward was taught by himſelfe and *Vincentio*, and by them beſt allowed of, to be the beſt ward to ſtand vpon in fight for life, either to aſſault the enemie, or ſtand and watch his comming, which ward it ſhould ſeeme he ventured his life vpon, but howſoeuer with all the fine Italienated skill *Ieronimo* had, *Cheeſe* with his Sword within two thruſtes ran him into the bodie and ſlue him. Yet the Italian teachers will ſay, that an Engliſhmã cannot thruſt ſtraight with a Sword, becauſe the hilt will not ſuffer him to put the forefinger ouer the Croſſe, nor to put the thumbe vpon the blade, nor to hold the pummell in the hand, whereby we are of neceſſitie to hold faſt the handle in the hand: by reaſon whereof we are driuen to thruſt both compaſſe and ſhort, whereas with the Rapier they can thruſt both ſtraight and much further then we can with the Sword, becauſe of the hilt: and theſe be the reaſons they make againſt the Sword.

FINIS.

BREF INSTRUCTIONS

VPÕ MY PRADOXES OF DEFENCE

for the true handling of all Mann^{r} of weapons together w^{t} the fower grownds & the fower gou^{r}nors wch gouernours are left out in my pradoxes w^{t}out the knowledge of wch no Man can fight ſaf

By *George Silver Gentleman*

[1599]

[Sloane MS. No. 376.]

TO THE READER.

FOr as much as in my padoxes of Defence I haue admonyshed Men to take heede of falſe teachers of Defence, yet once againe in theſe my bref inſtructions I do the lyke, becauſe Diuers have wryten books treating of the noble ſcience of Defence, wherin they rather teach offence then Defence, rather ſhewing men therby how to be ſlayne than to defend them ſelues frō the Dang^{r} of their enemys, as we may dayly ſe to the great grief & ouerthrowe of many braue gentlemen & gallent of o^{r} ever victorious nation of great brytaine,. And therfore for the great loue & Care y^{t} I haue for the well Doing & p^{r}ſ,vation of my Countrymen, ſeeing their Dayly ruens & vtter ou^{r}throw of Diu^{rs} gallant gent: & others wch truſt only to that Impfyt fyght of y^{t} Rapior, yeaſe although they Deyly ſe their owne ou^{r}throwes & ſlaughter therby, yet becaus they are trayned vp therin, they thinke & do fully pſwade them ſelues that ther is no fight ſo excelent & wher as amongſt div^{r}s other their oppynyons y^{t} leadeth them to this errous on of y^{t} cheifeſt is, becauſe ther be ſo many ſlayne w^{t} theſe weapons & therfore they hold them ſo exelent, but theſe thinges do cheifly happen, first because their fyght is Imprfyt for that they vse nether the prfyt gronds of true fyght, nether yet the 4 gou^r^nors w^t^out wch no man can fight saf, nether do they vse such other rules wch are required in the right vse of prfyt defence, and alßo their weapons for ye most prte beinge of an Imprfyt length, must of necessytie make an Imprfyt Defence because they Cannot vse them in due tyme & place, for had these valerous mynded men the right prfection of the true fyght w^t^ the short sword, & alßo of other weapons of prfyt length, I know y^t^ men would com saffer out of the field frō such bloddye bankets & that such would be their prfections her in, that it would saue many 100 mens lyues. But how should men lerne prfection out of such rules as are nothing els but very Imprfectiō it self. And as it is not fyt for a man wch desyreth ye clere lyght of the Day to go downe into the bottom of a deepe & Darke Dungion, belyvinge to fynd it there, so is it as Impossyble for men to fynd the prfyt knowledge of this noble science wher as in all their teachings every thinge is attempted & acted vpō Imprfyt rules, for ther is but one truth in all things, wch I wish very hartely were taught & practysed here amongst vs, & y^t^ those Imprfyt & murtherous kynde of falſe fyghts might be by them abolyshed. Leaue now to quaf & gull any Longer of that fylthy brynysh puddle, seeing yō may now drink of y^t^ fresh & clere sprynge.

O that men for their Defence would but geve their mynde to practise the true fyght in deed, & lerne to bere true brytish wards for thire defence, wch yf they had it in prfyt practyse, I speak it of myne owne knowledge y^t^ those Imprfyt Italyon Devyses w^t^ rapyor & ponyard would

would be clene caſt aſyde & of no account of al ſuch as blind offections do not lead beyond the bonds of reaſon. Therfore for the verye zealous & vnfayned loue y^t I beare vnto yor high & royal prſon my Cuntrymen pytting their cauſes y^t ſo many braue men ſhould be dayly murthered, & ſpoyled for want of true knowledge of this noble ſcience & not as ſom Imagyn to be, only ye excelence of ye rapior fyght, & wher as my padoxes of defence is to the moſt ſorte as a darke ryddle in many things ther in ſet downe, therfore I have now this ſecond tyme taken ſom paynes to write theſe few breef Inſtructions ther vppō wher by they may the better attayne to the truth of this ſcyence & laying open here all ſuch things as was ſom thinge Intrycat for them to vnd^r ſtand in my p^rdoxes & therfor y^t I haue the ful prfectiō & knowledge of the prfyt vſe of all mann^r of weapons, it Doth embolden me here in to wryte for the better Inſtructiō of the Vnſkylfull.

And I haue added to theſe my breef Inſtructions c^rtaine neceſarie admonytions wch I wiſh every man not only to know but alſo to obſ've & follow, Chiefly al ſuch as are deſyrous to enter into the right vſage & knowledge of their weapons, & alſo I haue thought it good to Annexe here vnto my p^rdoxes of Defence becauſe in theſe my bref Inſtructions, I haue referred ye reader to div^rs rules ther in ſet down.

This haue I wryten for an Infallible truth & a note of remembrance to o^r gallant gent: & others of o^r brave mynded Nation of great bryttaine, wch bere a mynde to defend them ſelues & to wyn honour in the feeld by their Actions of armes & ſyngle Combats.

And know y^t I write not this for vaineglorie, but out

of An entyre loue y^{t} I owe vnto my natyve Cuntrymen, as on who lamentith their Loſſes, ſorrye y^{t} ſo great an errour ſhould be ſo Carefully noryſhed as a ſ^{r}pant in their boſoms to their vtt^{r} confuſyõ, as of long tyme haue byn ſeene, wher as yf they would but ſeeke the truth her in they were eaſyly abolyſhed, therfore follow the truth & fly Ignorance.

And conſyd^{r} y^{t} learnyng hath no greater enemye than Ignorance, nether can the vnſkylfull euer Judge the truth of my arte to them unknowen, beware of raſh Judgment & accept my labours as thankfully as I beſtow them willingly, cenſuer me Juſtly, let no man Diſpiſe my worke herin Cauſeles, & ſo I refere my ſelf to the cenſuer of ſuch as are ſkylful herin & ſo I cõmyt yõ to the prtection of the almyghty Jehovah.

yo^{rs} in al loue & fryendly Affectiõ,

GEORGE SYLUER.

ADMONYTIONS

TO THE GENTLEMEN & BRAVE GALLANTS OF GREAT BRITAINE AGAINST QUARRELS & BRAULES WRITEN BY GEORGE SILUER. GENT.

WHeras I have declaired in my prdoxes of defence of the falſe teachinge of the noble ſcyence of defence vſed here by the Italyon fencers willing men therin to take heed how they truſted ther vnto w[t] ſuffytient reaſons & profs why.

And wher as ther was a booke wryten by Vincentio an Italiō teacher whoſe yll vſinge practiſes & vnſkylfull teaching were ſuch y[t] it hath coſt the lyves of many of o[r] brave gentlemen & gallants, the vnc[r]taintye of whoſe falſe teaching doth yet remayne to y[e] dayly murthering & ouer throw of many, for he & the reſt of them did not teach Defence but offence, as it doth playnlye appere by thoſe y[t] follow the ſame Imprfyt fyght according to their teaching or inſtructiōs by the orders from them prceedinge, for be the actors y[t] follow them neuer ſo prfyt or ſkylfull therin one or both of them are eyther ſore hurt or ſlaine in their Incountrs & fyghts, & yf they alledge yt we vſe it not rightly according to ye prfectiō therof, & therfore cannot defend or ſelues, to wch I anſwer yf themſelues had had any prfection therin, & that their teaching had byn a truth, themſelues would not have byn beaten & ſlayne in their fyghts, & vſing of their weapons, as they were.

And therfore I proue wher a man by their teaching can not be ſaf in his defence following their owne grounde of fyght then is their teaching offence & not defence, for in true fyght againſt the beſt no hurt can be don. And yf both haue the full prfection of true fyght, then the one will not be able to hurt the other at what prfyt weapon ſo ever.

For it cannot be ſayd yt yf a man go to the feld & cannot be ſure to defend him ſelf in fight & to com ſaf home, yf goid be not againſt him whither he fyght wt a man of ſkyll or no ſkil it may not be ſaid yt ſuch a man is Maſtr of the Noble ſcyence of defence, or that he hath the prfection of true fyght, for yf both haue the prfection of their weapons, yf by any Device, on ſhould be able to hurt the other, ther were no prfection in the fyght of weapons, & this firmely hold in yor mynd for a generall rule, to be the hayth & prfection of the true handling of al maner of weapons.

And alſo wheras yt ſaid Vincentio in ye ſame booke hath written diſcours of honour & honourable quarrels making many reaſons to prve meanes & wayes to enter ye feeld & cōbat, both for the lye & other diſgraces, al wch diabolicall devyces tendeth only to villayne & diſtruction as hurtynge, Maymynge & Murtheringe or kyllinge.

Annymating

Annymating yͤ mynds of yonge gentlemen & gallants to follow thoſe rules to maintaine their honors & credits, but the end ther of for the moſt prte is eyther kyllinge or hanginge or both to their vtter vndoinge & great gref of themſelues, & their friends, but then to late to call it againe. they conſyder not the tyme & place that we lyue in, nor do not throughly looke into the danger of the lawe til it be to late, & for that in diuers other cuntryes in theſe things they have a larger ſcope than we have in theſe our dayes.

Therfore it behoveth vs not upō euery abuſe offered wher by oʳ bloud ſhalbe Inflamed, or oʳ choler kindled pʳſently wᵗ the ſword or wᵗ the ſtabb, or by force of Armes to ſeeke Reuenge, wᶜʰ is the propre nature of wild beaſts in their rage ſo to do, being voyde of the vſe of reaſon, wᶜʰ thinge ſhould not be in Men of diſcreãtiō ſo much to Degenerate, but he yᵗ wil not endure an Iniurye, but will ſeeke revenge, then he ought to do it by Cyvill Order & prof, by good & holſom lawes, wᶜʰ are ordayned for ſuch Cauſes, wᶜʰ is a thinge far more fyt & requiſted in a place of ſo Cyvell a gouʳnment as we lyve in, then is the other, & who ſo followᵗ theſe my Admonycions ſhalbe accounted as valyent a Man as heyᵗ fyghteth & farr wyſer. for I ſee no reaſon why a Man ſhould adventure hys lyf & eſtate upō every tryfle, but ſhould rather put vp diu'ſ abuſes offered vnto him, becauſe it is agreeable both to the Lawes of god & oʳ Cuntrye.

Why ſhould not words be Anſwered wᵗ words againe, but yf a Man by his enemye be charged wᵗ blowes then may he Lawfully ſeeke the beſt meanes to defend him ſelf, & In ſuch a Caſe I hold it fyt to vſe his ſkyll & to ſhow his force by his Deeds, yet ſo, yᵗ his dealynge be not

not wt full Rygour to the others confusyon yf possyble it may be eschewed.

Also take heed how yō appoynt the field wt yor Enemye publickly because or Lawes do not prmyt yt, neyther appoint to meet him in pryvat sort lest yō wounding him he accuse yō of fellownye saying you have robbed him &c. Or he may laye companye closely to Murther you & then to report he dyd yt him self valyently in the feeld.

Also take heed of thyne Enemyes Stratagems, lest he fynd Meanes to make yō to looke a syde vpō somthing, or cause yō to shew whether yō have on a p'vye Coate, & so when yō Looke from him, he hurt or kyll you.

Take not armes vpō euery light occasyon, let not one fryend vpon a word or a tryfle violate another but let ech man zealously embrace fryendshyp, & turne not famylyaritie into strangnes, kyndnes into mallice, nor loue into hatred, norish not these strange & vnnaturall Alterations.

Do not wyckedly resolue one to seeke the others ou'throwe, do not confyrme to end thy Mallice by fyght because for the most prte yt endeth by Death.

Consyder when these things were most vsed in former Ages they sought not so much by envye the ruen & distruction on of another, they never tooke tryall by sword but in defence of Innocencye to maintayne blotless honour.

Do not vpon Euery tryfle make an Action of revenge, or of Defyance.

Go not into the feeld wt thy fryend at his Intreatye to take his prte but first know ye mann' of ye quarrell how Justly or vniustlye it grow, & do not ther in maintaine wronge

Facsimile page of the MS. of "Bref Instructions."
(Sloane MS. No. 376.)
(Actual size.)

Vpon, yf then he shal sodenlye rayse vp the point
of his pyke wt his other hand & come to thrust at you
then in the meetinge of his point or his cominge
in, sodenlye lyfte vp the point of yor pyke, wt your
hand synglo, & so thrust him in the bellye wt your
pyke, & fly out therewt.

Or els you may stand vpo yor ward, & not lyft
vp yor pykes point, but breake his thrust by cros
singe the point of his pyke wt the myddle of yor
pyke by raysinge vp yor hand wt the butt end of
yor pyke above yor hed, & so bringe over his
point wt yor staf to the other syde as for example,

yf he lye wt his hand & point towarde the left
2. syde of yor bodye, then sodenlye bear his point
over strongly towarde yor right syde.

yf he lye wt his hand & point towarde yor right
syde, then bear his point towarde yor left syde
& ther vpon gather vp yor pyke wt yor other hand
& thrust at him & fly out.

yf he contynue his fyght at his point above
& he lye at yor pyke length hyer or lyer wt your
hand & point so, yt yo may make yor thrust at
his face or bodye, wt yor point directly towarde
his face, holdinge yor pyke wt both yor hande
on yor staf, yor hinder hande wt yor knuckles
upwarde, & yor formost hand wt yor knuckles
downwarde, & ther stayinge yor pyke & faulsinge
at his face wt yor point as nere his face as
you may, then sodenlye make out yor thrust
synglo

wronge againſt ryght, but examyne the cauſe of the contravercye, & yf ther be reaſon for his rage to lead him to y^{t} mortall reſolution.

Yet be the cauſe neuer ſo Juſt, go not w^{t} him neyther further nor ſuffer him to fight yf poſſyble it may by any meanes be otherwyſe ended & wyll him not to enter into ſo dangerous an action, but leue it till neccefytie requireth it.

And this I hold to be the beſt Courſe for it is fooliſhnes & endleſſe troble to caſt a ſtone at euerye Dogge y^{t} barks at you. this noble ſcyence is not to cauſe on man to abuſe another iniuriouſlye but to vſe it in their neceſſyties to defend them in their Juſt Cauſes & to maintaine their honour & Credits.

Therfore flye al raſhnes, pryde, & doynge of Iniurie all foule faults & errours herin, p^{r}ſume not on this, & therbye to think it lawfull to offer Iniurye to Anye, think not yo^{r}ſelf Invincible, but conſyder y^{t} often a verye wretch hath kylled a taule man, but he y^{t} hath humanytie, the more skylful he is in this noble ſcience, the more humble, modeſt, & V^{r}tuous he ſhould ſhew him ſelf both in ſpeech & Action, no lyer, no vaunter nor quarreller, for theſe are the cauſes of Wounds, Diſhonour & Death.

Yf you talke w^{t} great men of honourable qualitie w^{t} ſuch chiefly haue regarde to frame yor ſpeeches & Anſwer ſo reverent, y^{t} a fooliſh word, or froward Anſwer geve no occaſyon of offence for often they breed Deadly hatred, Cruell murthers & extreem ruens &c.

Ever ſhun al occaſyons of quarrels, but marſhall men cheiflye generals & great cōmanders ſhould be exelent skylfull in the noble ſcience of defence, therby to be able to answer quarrels, Combats & Chalenges in Defence of their prince & Cuntry.

Vale.

Bref Instructions vpō my pradoxes of Defence for the true handlyng of all Mann^{r} of weapons together w^{t} the fower grownds & the fower gou^{r}nors wch gouernours are left out in my pradoxes w^{t}out the knowledge of wch no Man can fight saf.

Cap. I.

The fower grownds or principls of ye true fyght at all manner of Weapons are these 4, viz.	1.	*Judgment*
	2.	*Distance*
	3.	*Tyme*
	4.	*Place.*

THe reason wherof these 4 grownds or p^{r}nciples be the fyrst & cheefest, are the followinge, because through Judgment, yō kepe yor dystance, through Distance yō take yor Tyme, through Tyme yō safly wyne or gayne the Place of yor adu^{r}sarie, the Place beinge woon or gayned yō haue tyme safly eyther to stryke, thrust, ward, cloze, grype, slyp or go back, in the wch tyme yor enemye is disapoynted to hurt yō, or to defend himself, by reason that he hath lost his true Place, the reason y^{t} he hath lost his True place is by the length of Tyme

Tyme through the numbs of his feet, to wch he is of neceſſytie Dryven to yt wilbe Agent.

The 4 gournors are thoſe yt follow.

1. The fyrſt gournor is Judgment wch is to know when yor Adverſarie can reach you, & when not, & when yō can do the lyke to him, & to know by the goodnes or badnes of his lyinge, what he can do, & when & how he can pforme it.

2. The ſecond gournor is Meaſure. Meaſure is the better to know how to make yor ſpace true to defend yor ſelf, or to offend yor enemye.

3. The third & fourth gourners is a twyfold mynd when
yō preſs in on yor enemye, for as yō have a mynd to go
4. forwarde, ſo yō muſt haue at yt inſtant a mynd to fly
backwarde vpō any action yt ſhalbe offered or don by yor
adurſarie.

Certaine general rules wch muſt be obſyved in yt prſyt vſe of al kynde of weapons.

Cap. 2.

1. FYrſt when you com into the feeld to encounter wt yor Enemy, obſyve wel the ſcope, Evennes & vneunnes of yor grounde, put yorſelf in redynes wt yor weapon, before yor enemye Com wtin diſtance, ſet the ſvnn in his face travers yf poſſible yō can ſtill remembrynge yor gournors.

2. Let al yor lyinge be ſuch as ſhal beſt like yorſelf, euer conſyderinge out what fyght yor Enemye chargeth yō, but be ſure to kepe yor diſtance, ſo yt nether hed, Armes,

"Put in his foot," i.e. advance.

hands, body, nor legges be w^{t}in hys reach, but y^{t} he must fyrst of necessytie put in his foote or feet, at wch tyme yō haue the Choyse of iij Actions by the wch yō may endang^{r} him & go free yo^{r}self.

"His cominge in." It must be remembered that in Silver's time the lunge was unknown, at least to English fencers, & the only movements of the feet were "passes" and "traverses," which with "slips" constituted a great part of the defence as well as of the attack. "Passes" were steps either forwards or backwards and the "traverses" were steps in a lateral direction. "Slips" were little short steps either lateral or backwards. These movements were also much used in feints of attack.

1. The fyrst is to strike or thrust at him, at y^{t} instant when he haue gayned yō the place by his cominge in
2. The second is to ward, & Aft^{r} to strike or thrust from y^{t}, remembringe yor gou^{r}nors
3. The thyrd is to slippe alyttle backe & to strike or thrust after hym.

but euer remember y^{t} in the fyrst motion of your Adversarye towarde yō, y^{t} yō slyde a lyttle back so shall yō be p^{r}pred in due tyme to prforme anye of the iij Actions Aforesaid, by disappointynge him of his true place, whereby yō shall saflye defend yo^{r}selfe & endanger him.

remember also y^{t} yf through fear or polysye, he strike or thrust short, & ther w^{t} go back, or not go back, follow him vpon yor twofold gou^{r}nors, so shall yor warde & slype be prformed in lyke mann^{r} as before, & yo^{r}self stil be saf.

Kepe yor dystance & suffer not yor adu^{r}sarie to wyn 3.
or gayne the place of you, for yf he shall so do, he may endanger to hurt or kyll you.

Know y^{t} the place is, when on may stryke or thrust home w^{t}out puttinge in of his foot.

"To wyn or gayne the place;" i.e. to come within striking distance.

Yt may be obiected against thys last ground, y^{t} men do often strike & thrust at the half sword & yet the same is prfytly defended, where to I answer y^{t} that defence is prfytly made by reason y^{t} the warder hath his true space before the stryker or thruster is in his force or entred into his action.

Therfore

Therfore alwaies do p^{r}vent both blow & thruſt, the blow by true ſpace, & the thruſt by narrow ſpace y^{t} is true croſſinge it before the ſame com into their full force, other wyſe the hand of the Agent beinge as ſwyſt as ye hand of the patient, the hand of ye Agent beinge the fyrſt mou^{r}, muſt of neceſſytie ſtrike or thruſt y^{t} prte of ye patient wch ſhalbe ſtryken or thruſt at becauſe the tyme of y^{t} hand to the tyme of ye hand, beinge of lyke ſwyftnes the fyrſt mou^{r} hath ye aduantage.

“Space” is the diſtance which the ſword blade has to traverſe in changing from one poſition to another: thus from “medium” to “quarte” or “tierce” would be a “narrow ſpace,” while from “tierce” to “ſeptime” or from “ſeconde” to “quarte” would be a very “wyde ſpace.”

4. When yor enemy ſhal preſs vpon you, he wilbe Open in one place or other, both at ſyngal & dubble weapon, or at the leaſt he wilbe to weake in his ward vpon ſuch p^{r}ſſinge, then ſtrike or thruſt at ſuch open or weakeſt prte y^{t} yo ſhal fynd neereſt.

5. When yō attempt to wyn the place, do it vpon gard, remembringe yor gou^{r}nors, but when he p^{r}ſſeth vpō yō & gayneth yō The place, then ſtrike or thruſt at him in his cōmynge in,

A time hit or thruſt.

Or yf he ſhal ſtryke or thruſt at yō, then Ward it, & ſtryke or thruſt at him from yor warde, & fly backe Inſtantly accordinge to yor gou^{r}nors, ſo ſhall yō eſcape ſaflie, for that the fyrſt Motion of the feete backwarde is more ſwyſt, then the firſt motion of the feet forwarde, wher by yor regreſſyon wilbe more ſwyfter, then his courſe in prgreſſyon to Anoye you, the reaſon is, that in the fyrſt motyon of his prgreſſyon his Numb^{r} & Waight is greater then yo^{rs} are, in yor firſt motyon of yor regreſſyon, neu^{r}theleſs al men knowe that the cō-tynual courſe of the feet forwarde is more ſwyſt then the Contynuall Courſe of ye feet backwards.

Parry and Ripoſte. Silver is very careful to emphaſiſe the neceſſity of “flying backe,” i.e. getting away, immediately after an attack, whether it be ſucceſsful or otherwiſe.

6. yf yor enemye lye in varyable fyght, & ſtryke or thruſt at yō then be ſure to kepe yor Diſtance & ſtrike

Time hits & thruſts.

or thruſt at ſuch open prte of him as are neereſt vnto you, viz, at the hand, Arme, hed, or legg of him, & go back w^{t} all,

yf ij men fight at varyable fyght, & yf w^{t}in diſtance, 7.
they muſt both be hurt, for in ſuch fight they Cannot make a true Croſſe, nor haue tyme trulye to Judge, by reaſon y^{t} the ſwyft motyon of the hand, beinge a ſwyfter moue^{r}, then the eye Deceyveth the eye, at what weapon ſoeuer yō ſhal fyght w^{t} all, as in my pradoxes of defence in the chapter therof doth appere.

The "grype" is the ſeizing of the ſword-hilt with the left hand,—for this purpoſe a "guanto da preſa," or gripping gauntlet with the palm protected with fine mail, was ſometimes uſed. To "indirect" is to either manœuvre or force him from the true line of direction.

Looke to the grype of yor Enemye, & vpō his ſlype 8.
take ſuch warde as ſhal beſt ſyt your hand, from wch warde ſtrike or thruſt, ſtil remembrynge yor gouernors,

yf yō can Indirect yor enemye at any kynde of weapon, 9.
then yō haue the aduantage, becauſe he muſt moue his feet to direct him ſelf Againe, & yō in the meane tyme may ſtrike or thruſt at him, & fly out faſt, before he can offer anything at you, his tyme wilbe ſo longe.

A Demi-volte.

When you ſhall Ward blow or thruſt, made at yor 10.
right or left prte, w^{t} any kynd of weapon, rememb^{r} to Draw yor hynde foot a lyttle c^{r}culerlye, from that prte to wch the ſame ſhalbe made, wher by yō ſhall make yor defence the more prfyt, & ſhal ſtand the more Apt to ſtrike or thruſt from yt.

A

A declaration of al the 4 generall fyghts to be vſed wt the ſword at dubble or ſyngle, longe or ſhort, & wt Certaine pticuler rules to them Annexed.

Cap. 3.

1. OPen fyght is to Carrye yor hand & hylt a loft aboue yor hed, eyther wt poynt vpright, or point backwards wch is beſt, yet vſe that wch yō ſhall fynd moſt apteſt, to ſtrike, thruſt, or ward.

The "Guardia alta" of Marozzo & "Terza guardia" of Viggiani.

2. Gardant fyght in genrall is of ij ſorts, ye fyrſt is true gardant fyght, wch is eyther prfyt or Imprfyt.

A "hanging" guard. "True gardant" is a High Prime.

The prfyt is to carry yor hand & hylt aboue yor hed wt yor poynt doune to wards yor left knee, wt yor ſword blade ſomewhat neer yor bodye, not bearing out your poynt, but rather declynynge in a lyttle towards yor ſaid knee, yt yor enemye croſe not yor poynt & ſo hurt you, ſtand bolt vpright in this fyght, & yf he offer to preſſe in then bere yor hed & body a lyttle backwarde.

Command.

The Imprfyt is when yō bere yor hand & ſword hylt prfyt hayth aboue yor hed, as aforeſayd but leanynge or ſtoopinge forwarde wt yor body & therby yor ſpace wilbe to Wyde on both ſyds to defend the blow ſtryken at the left ſyde of yor hed or to wyde to defend a thruſt from the ryght ſyde of the body,

To ſtand with the body leaning forward is an "imperfect" poſition.

Alſo it is Imprfyt, yf yō bere yor hand & hylt as aforeſayd, berynge yor poynt to farr out from yor knee, ſo yt yor enemy May Croſs, or ſtrike Aſyde yor poynt, & therby endanger you,

The

"Baſtard gardant" is a kind of high ſeconde, but more central.

The ſecond is baſtard gardant fyght wch is to Carrye yor hand & hylt below yor hed, breſt hye or lower w^{t} yor poynt downwarde towarde yor left foote, this baſtard gardant ward is not to be vſed in fyght, ecept it be to Croſſe yor enemyes Ward at his comynge in to take the grype of him or ſuch other advantage, as in diu^{r}s placs of y^{e} ſword fyght is ſet forth.

"Forehand ward" is a medium guard.

Cloſe fyght is when yō Croſs at ye half ſword eyther 3.
aboue at forehand ward y^{t} is w^{t} poynt hye, & hande & hylt lowe, or at true or baſtard gardant ward w^{t} both yor poynts doun.

Cloſe is all mann^{r} of fyghts wherin yō have made a 4.
true Croſe at the half ſword w^{t} yor ſpace very narrow & not Croſt, is alſo cloſe fyght.

The Italian terms were imperfectly underſtood in England at the end of the XVIth century, & Silver has evidently miſconſtrued them.

Variable fyght is al other mann^{r} of lyinge not here before ſpoken of, wher of theſe 4 that follow are the cheefeſt of them.

"Quinta guardia" of Capo Ferro.

Stocata: wch is to lye w^{t} yor right legge forwarde, w^{t} (1.)
yor ſword or rapior hylt back on the out ſyde of yor right thygh w^{t} yor poynt forewarde to ward yor enemye, w^{t} yor dagg^{r} in yor other hand extendinge yor hand to wards the poynt of yor rapior, holdinge yor dagg^{r} w^{t} ye poynt vpright w^{t} narrow ſpace betweene yor rapior blade, & the nayles of yor dagg^{r} hand, kepynge yor rapior poynt back behind yor dagg^{r} hand yf poſſyble,

"Prima guardia" of Capo Ferro, "Guardia alta" of Alfieri, & "Guardia di becha poſſa" of Marozzo.

Or he may lye wyde below vnd^{r} his dagg^{r} w^{t} his rapior poynt doun towards his enemyes foote, or w^{t} his poynt fourth w^{t} out his dagg^{r}.

"Quarta guardia" of Alfieri.

Imbrocata: is to lye w^{t} yor hylt hyer then yor hed, beringe yor knuckles vpwarde, & yor point depending towarde yor Enemys face or breſt.

Mountanta: is to Carrye yor rapior pummell in the palm

palm of yor hand reſting it on yor lyttle fynger w^{t} yor hand belowe & ſo movntynge it vp a loft, & ſo to com in w^{t} a thruſt vpō yor Enemyes face or breſt, as out of ye Imbrocata.

4. Paſſata; is eyther to paſs w^{t} ye Stocata, or to carrye yor ſword or rapior hylt by yor right flanke, w^{t} yor poynt directly againſt yor Enemyes belly, w^{t} yor left foote forwarde, extendinge fourth yor dagg^{r} hand w^{t} the poynt of yor dagger forwarde as yō do yor ſword, w^{t} narrow ſpace between yor ſword & dagg^{r} blade, & ſo to make yor paſſage vpon him,

Alſo any other kynd of varyable fyght or lyeinge whatſoeuer a man can deviſe not here expreſſed, is cōtayned vnder this fight.

The "ſhort ſyngle ſword fight" was a fight with a one-hand ſword, and without the aſſiſtance of a defenſive weapon in the left hand. The "ſword dubble" is any kind of ſingle-hand ſword aſſiſted by a defenſive weapon in the other.

Of the ſhort ſyngle ſword fyght againſt the lyke weapon.

Cap. 4.

1. YF yor enemye lye a loft, eyther in open or true gardant fight, & then ſtrike at the left ſyde of yor hed or body yor beſt ward to defend yor ſelf, is to bere it w^{t} true gardant ward, & yf he ſtrike & com in to the cloze, or to take the grype of you yō may then ſafly take the grype of him as it appereth in the chapter of the grype, *A high prime.*

2. but yf he do ſtrike & not com in, then inſtantly vpō yor ward, vncroſe & ſtrike him either on the right or left ſyde of ye hed, & fly out inſtantly. *A direct "ripoſte."*

"Fly out" ſuggeſts a lateral movement of the feet, but might alſo mean a backward one.

3. Yf yō bere this w^{t} forhand ward, be ſure to ward his blowe, or kepe yor diſtance, otherwyſe he ſhall decue

you wt euery falſe, ſtil endangeringe yor hed, face, hand, Armes, bodye, & bendynge knee, wt blow or thruſt. Therfore kepe well yor dyſtance, bęcauſe yō can very hardly deſerne (being wt in dyſtance), by wch ſyde of yor ſword he will ſtryke, nor at wch of thoſe prts aforeſayd, becauſe the ſwyft motion of ye hand deceyveth the eye,

A ſimilar guard is favoured by ſome modern Auſtrian ſabre players.

yf he lye a loft & ſtrike as aforeſaid at yor head, yō may 4.
endanger him yf yō thruſt at his hand, hilt, or Arme, turninge yor knuckles dounwarde, but fly back wt all in the inſtant yt yō thruſt,

A time thruſt in "quarte" at the ſword hand.

A "quarte" parry, followed by "ripoſte" or "grip."

yf he lye a loft as aforeſaid, & ſtrike a loft at the left 5.
ſyde of yor hed, yf yō wil ward his blow wt forehand ward, then be ſure to kepe yor diſtance, except he com ſo crtaine that yō be ſure to ward his blow, at wch tyme yf he com in wt all, yō may endanger him from yt ward, eyther by blow, thruſt or grype,

yf he lye a loft & yō lye a lowe wt yor ſword in the 6.
varyable ſyght, then yf yō offer to ward his blow made at yor hed, wt true gardant ward yor tyme wilbe to longe Due in tyme to make a ſure ward, for that it is bettr to bere it wt forehand ward, but be ſure to kepe yor diſtance, to make him com in wt his feet, wher by his tyme wilbe to longe to do yt he intendeth.

yf ij Men fight both vpō open fyght he yt firſt break- 7.
eth his diſtance, yf he attempt to ſtryke at the others hed, ſhalbe ſurely ſtryken on the hed himſelf, yf the patient Agent ſtrike ther at in his Comynge in, & ſlyp a lyttle back wt all, for yt ſlydinge back maketh an indirection, wherby yor blow Croſſeth his hed, & maketh a true ward for yor owne, this will yt be, becauſe of his length of tyme in his cōmynge in,

A time hit with "oppoſition."

Alſo

8. Also yf ij fyght vpon open fyght, it is better for the patient to strike home strongly at the Agents hed, when the said Agent shal press vpon him to wyn the place then to thrust, because the blow of the patient is not only hurtful to the Agent, but it also maketh a true Crose to defend his owne hed,

9. yf he charge yō a loft, out of the open or true gardant fyght, yf yō answer him wt ye Imprfyt gardant fyght, wt yor body leanynge forwarde, yor space wilbe to wyde on both syde to make a true ward in due tyme, & yor arme And body wilbe to neere vnto him, so that wt the bending in of his body wt the tyme of hand & foote, he may take the grype of you,

but yf yō stand vpright in true gardant fyght, then he cannot reach to take the grype of you, nor otherwise to offend yō yf you kepe yor distance, wtout puttinge in of his foote or feete wherin his number wilbe to great, & so his tyme wilbe to longe, & yō in that tyme may by puttinge in of yor body take the grype of him, yf he press to com in wt vsing only yor hand, or hand & foote, & ther vpon yō may stryke or thrust wt yor sword & fly out wt all accordinge to yor governors, se more of this, in the chapter of the grype.

"Number wilbe to great," i.e. will have to make too many steps or passes.

10. yf he wil stil prsse forcibly a loft vpō you, Charginge yō out of the open fyght or true gardant fyght, Intendinge to hurt yō in the face or hed, or to take the grype of yō Against such a on, you must vse both gardant & open fyght, wherby vpon euery blow or thrust that he shall make at you, you may from yor wards, strike or thrust him on the face hed or bodye as it appeareth more at large in the 5th Chapter of these my Instructions.

11. yf yō fyght wt on yt standeth only vpon his gardant fyght *A variety of*

both play only vpon dubble hand, then his blade wch is of cõvenyent length agreeing w^t^ his stature y^t^ hath it, wch is according with the length of the measure of his syngle swordblade, hath the advantage of ye sword y^t^ is to long for ye stature of the contrarye prtye, because he can crose & vncrose, strike & thrust, cloze & grype in shorter tyme than the other can.

Of the short staf fyght, being of cõvenient length, against ye like weapon.

Cap. 11.

THE short staf hath iiij wards, y^t^ is ij w^t^ ye point vp, & ij w^t^ the poynt doune,

At these weapons euer lye so that yõ may be able to thrust syngle & dubble, & to ward, strike, or thrust in due tyme, so shal yor enemye, yf he fyght only vpõ dubble hand be driuen of necessitie, seeking to wyn the place, to gayne yõ the place wher by yõ may safly hurt him, & go free yor self by reason of yor distance, & when yõ shal seeke to wyn the place vpon him he shal not be able to gaine the place vpon you, nor to kepe the place frõ you wher by he shal eyther be hurt, or in great danger of hurt, by reason of yor large reach, true place & distance, yor fight being truly handled keeping it self from Cloze & grype. 1.

And in like sort shal it be betweene two, wch shal play vpon the best, y^t^ is, yf they play both dubble & syngle handed. 2.

yf yõ fynd yor self to strong for yor adu^r^sarie in any mann^r^ of ward, whether the same be aboue or belowe, put by his staf w^t^ force, & then strike or thrust from it, 3.

but

Facsimile page of the MS. of "Bref Instructions."

(Actual size.)

uncertaine and in al your fyght wth this weapon
to make yor space narrow, whether it be against
4. the staff or byll, so that what so ever he shal do
against you, you shal still make yor ward before
he be in his ful force to offend you/

Also yf you can make a crosse at the end of his byll
5. wth the end of yor byll, then sodainly wth the end of
yor byll snatch his byll end, strongly towarde
you, & therwthall indirect his byl end, & forci//
bly run up yor byl end to his hande, so have you
the lyke advantage as abovesaid, wherof I spake
of running up towarde his hande/

Yf he lye alowe wth his byl end, then yf you can
6. put yor byll end, in at the end of his byll, & strong//
ly put downe his byl staff, wth yor byl end, bea//
ringe it flat, then you may presently run up yor
byll end single handed, to his hande & fly out
therwth, so shal you hurt him in the hand & save
yor selfe

The lyke may you do wth yor byll against
7 the short staff, yf you can presse it downe in the
lyke sort, but yf he have a longer staff, then run
up dubble handed, wth both hande upon yor byll, wch
thinge you may safely do, because you are in yor
strengthe, & have taken him in the weake parte of
his staff/

Yf he lye hyghe wth his byll end, then put up
8 yor byll end under his, & cast his byll out to the
syde that you shal fynd fittest/ so have you the ad//
vantage to thrust or stryke at him, & fly out/

Or yf you cast his byll hand out of the right
lyne

4. but yf yō fynd him to strong for yō vpō hys blowes from a loft, so y^{t} yō can hardly bere them vpon yor ward, then when he stryketh in a loft at yor hed, & by hys maine strength would beat doune yor staf, & so geue yō a hurt before yō shalbe able to com againe into yor ward,

Against such a on giue the slypp in this sort, sodainly dray back the hyer prte of yor body a lyttle & yor for most foote w^{t} all, & slyp in the poynt of yor staf vnd^{r} his staf, & thrust single at him, & fly out w^{t} all, so shal you be sure to hyt him & go out free,

5. yf he lye a loft w^{t} his staf, then lye yō w^{t} your hind^{r} hand alowe, w^{t} yor poynt vptowards his staf making yor space narrow because yō may crose hys staf to ward his blow before it com in ful force, & then strongly & sodainlye indirect his poynt, & so thrust at him syngle, the wch yō may do before he can remoue his feet, by reason of the swyftnes of yor hand & fly out ther w^{t}, do this for both syds of ye hed yf cause require yt, so shal yō saue both yor hed, body, and al prts, for yor vpp^{r} prts are garded, & yor lower prts to farr out of his reach.

6. yf he lye a lowe w^{t} his poynt doune, then lye yō w^{t} yor poynt doune also, w^{t} yor formost hand lowe & yor hind^{r} most hand hye, so y^{t} yō may crose his staf, & do in al things as is before said in the other

7. yf he lye vpō the thrust then lye yō w^{t} yor space narrow lying vp or doune w^{t} yor poynt in such sort as you may crose his staf, & therby yō shal be able to put or beat by his thrust before it be in ful force, & then strike or thrust, euer remembring yor gouernors.

yf vpon this any wil obiect y^{t} yf this be true, then it is is in vaine to ſtrike, or thruſt, becauſe he y^{t} doth it is ſtil in danger, this doubt is anſwered in the ſhort ſingle ſword fight, in the 12th ground thereof

Yf yor adu^{r}ſarie ſtrike a loft at any ſyde of yor hed 8.
or body, ward it w^{t} yor point vp & making yor ſpace ſo narrow y^{t} yō may croſe his ſtaf before it com in ful force bearing or beating doune his blow ſtrongly, back againe towards y^{t} ſyde y^{t} he ſtryketh in at you, & out of y^{t} ward, then Inſtantly, eyther ſtrike frō y^{t} ward, turning back yor ſtaf, & ſtrike him on y^{t} ſyde of the hed y^{t} is next yor ſtaf,

Or lyſt vp yor ſtaf againe, & ſo ſtrike him on the hed or body, or thruſt at his body dubble or ſyngle, as yō may find yor beſt aduantage ever in holding yor ſtaf, let ther be ſuch convenient ſpace between yor hands, wher in you ſhal fynd yor ſelf apteſt to ward, ſtrike or thruſt to yor beſt lyking

Yf yō play w^{t} yor ſtaf w^{t} yor left hand before & yor 9.
right hand back behind, as many men do fynd them ſelues moſt apteſt when y^{t} hand is before, & yf yor aduerſarie vpō his blowe com in to take the cloze of you, when yō fynd his ſtaf croſt w^{t} yo^{rs} neere his hand then ſodainlye ſlyp vp yor right hand cloſe to the hind^{r} ſyde of yor formoſt hand, & p^{r}ſently looſing yor for muſt hand & put it vnd^{r} your owne ſtaf, & then croſe or put by his ſtaf ther w^{t} & w^{t} yor hand take hold of his ſtaf in ſuch ſort y^{t} yor lyttle fyng^{r} be towards the poynt of his ſtaf, & yor thumb & fore fing^{r} towards his hands, & p^{r}ſently w^{t} yor right hand mount ye point of yor owne ſtaf caſting the point thereof back ouer yor right ſhold^{r}, w^{t} yor knuckles doun wards, & yor nayles vpwards, & ſo ſtabb him in

the

the body or face w^t the hind^r end of y^r staf, but be sure to stabb him at his cōmyng in, whether yō catch his staf or not, for somtymes his staf will lye so farr out y^t vpon his cōmyng in yō cannot reach it, then catch y^t arme in his comynge in wch he shal first put forth w^t in yor reach, but be sure to stabb, for his staf can do yō no hurt, and having so don, yf yō fynd yor self to strong for him, strike vp his heeles, yf to weake fly out.

10. The like must yō do yf yō play w^t yor right hand before, & yor left hand back behind, but y^t yō neede not to slyde forth yor left hand, because yor right hand is in the right place of yor staf alredye to vse in y^t action, but then yō must displace yor left hand to take hold of his staf, or the grype as is a foresaid, & to vse the stabb as is aboue said,

11. yf both lye a loft as aforesaid, & play w^t ye left hand before, yf he strike at the Ryght syde of yor hed or body then must yō crose his staf before his blow be in ful force, by making yor space narrow, & then strike it strongly back againe towards his left syde, & from y^t ward yō may turne back yor staf & strike him backwards ther w^t on the left syde of the hed, or lyft vp yor staf & strike him on the right or left syde of the hed, body, or arme, or thrust him in the body, the lyke blowes or thrusts may you make at him whether he strike or thrust, having put by his staf, remembring yor gou^rnors.

The like ord^r must yō vse in playing with the right hand before,

12. but yf he thrust at yō cōtynually then euer have a speciall care to cōsyder, whether he lye a loft or be-lowe,

lowe, & do continually thruſt at yō ther from, then looke that yō euer lye ſo y^t yō make yor ſpace ſo narrow vpon him, y^t yō be ſure to croſe his ſtaf w^t yo^{rs}, & put it before it be in full force, and frō y^t ward, thruſt at him ſyngle or dubble as yō fynd it beſt, & yf he remembr not to fly back at y^t inſtant when he thruſteth it wilbe to late for him to avoyd any thruſt y^t yō ſhal make at him,

Of the ſhort ſtaf fyght againſt the longe ſtaf.
Cap. 12.

YF yō haue a ſtaf of the cōvenient length 1.
againſt a ſtaf of longer length than is cōvenient then make yor ſpace narrow, & ſeeke not to offend vntil yō haue ſtrongly & ſwyftly put by his point the wch yō ſhal w^t eaſe accompliſh, by reaſon of yor narrow ſpace & yor force, then ſtrike or thruſt as yō ſhal thinke beſt.

This ſhort ſtaf fight againſt ye longe ſtaf is don in 2.
the ſame ſort that ſhort ſtaf fight to ſhort ſtaf is don, but y^t the man w^t the ſhort ſtaf muſt alwaies remembr to kepe a narrow ſpace vpon ye long ſtaf, wher ſo euer the longe ſtaf ſhal lye, Hye or lowe, cōtinually make yor ſpace narrow vpō him, ſo ſhal yō be ſure yf he ſtrike or thruſt at yō, to take the ſame before it be into his full force & by reaſon y^t yor force is more w^t yor ſhort ſtaf than his can be at the poynt of his longe ſtaf, yō ſhal caſt his ſtaf ſo farr out of y^e ſtreit lyne w^t yor ſhort ſtaf, y^t yō may ſafly enter in w^t yor feet, & ſtrike or thruſt home at him.

Yet this p^r^ſent ſhift he hath at y^t inſtant, he may 3.
ſlypp

ſlypp back his ſtaf in his hands, wch tyme is ſwyfter then yor feet in cōmynge forwarde, wher by he wil haue his ſtaf as ſhort as yo^{rs}, yet by reaſon y^{t} at ye firſt yō caſt his ſtaf ſo farr out of the right lyne, that yō had tyme to enter in w^{t} yor feet, yō ſhal then be ſo neere him, y^{t} yō may make narrow ſpace vpō him againe, ſo y^{t} he ſhal haue no tyme to ſlyp forwarde his ſtaf agayne in his former place, nor to go back w^{t} his feet, & ſo to recou^{r} the hind^{r} end of his ſtaf againe, becauſe yf he ſlyp forth his ſtaf to ſtrike or thruſt at you, that may yō ſafly defend becauſe of your narrow ſpace vpō him, & ther w^{t} al yō may ſtrike or thruſt him frō yor warde, eyther at ſyngle or dubble,

4. but yf he wil go back w^{t} his feet thinking by y^{t} meanes to recou^{r} the whole length of hys ſtaf againe, y^{t} can he not do in cōvenyent tyme because the tyme of yor hand is ſwyft^{r} than ye tyme of his feet, by reaſon wherof yō may ſtrike or thruſt him in his goyng back.

5. Againe it is to be remembred in y^{t} tyme y^{t} yō keepe him at y^{t} bay, vpō the drawing in of his ſtaf, the hind^{r} end therof lying ſo farr back behind him wilbe ſo trobbleſom vnto him, that he can make no prfyt fight againſt yō & cōmonly in his drawing in of his ſtaf it wilbe to ſhort to make true fight against you, nether to offend yō nor defend him ſelf.

6. yf he attempt the Cloze w^{t} yō then ſtabb him w^{t} the hind^{r} end of yor ſtaf as is ſaid in ye fyght of ye ij ſhort ſtaves of cōvenyent length, in the 9th ground therof

Note. Rememb^{r} y^{t} at Morris pyke, forreſt byll, longe ſtaf & two hand ſword, y^{t} yō lye in ſuch ſort vpō yor wards y^{t} yō may both ward, ſtrike, & thruſt, both dubble & syngle, & then returne to yo[r] former wards slyps & lyinge againe & then are yō as yō wer before

The like fight is to be vsed w[t] y[e] Javelen, prtyson, halbard, black byll, battle Axe, gleve, half pyke &c.

Off the fight of the forrest byll against the like weapon & against the staf.

Cap: 13.

THE forrest byl haue the fyght of the staf but 1.
y[t] it hath iiij wards more w[t] the hed of the byll, y[t] is one to bere it vpwards, another to beat it dounwards so y[t] the carrage of yo[r] byll hed be w[t] the edge neyther vp nor doune but syde wyse.

The other ij wards are on to cast his byl hed towards the ryght syde, thother towards y[e] left syde.

And vpon ei[r] on of these wards or catches run vp to his hands w[t] the hed of yo[r] byll & then by reason y[t] yō haue put his staf out of y[e] right lyne, yō may catch at his hed neck arme or leggs &c w[t] y[e] edge of yo[r] byll, & hook or pluck him strongly to you & fly out w[t]all.

Yf yō cast his staf so farr out y[t] yo[r] byll slyde not 2.
vp to his hands, then yō may safly run in slyding yo[r] hands w[t]in one yard of y[e] hed of yo[r] byll, & so w[t] yo[r] byl in one hand take him by y[e] legg w[t] the blade of yo[r] byll & pluck him to yō & w[t] yo[r] other hand defend yo[r] self from his gryps yf he offer to grype w[t] you.

Yf you fight byll to byll do the like in al respects 3.
as w[t] y[e] staf in yo[r] fyght, for yo[r] byll fight & staf fyght is

is al one, but only for the defence & offence w^{t} the hed of ye byll, & wher y^{e} ſtaf man vpō the cloze yf he vſe y^{e} ſtabb w^{t} the butt end of his ſtaf, the byll man at y^{t} tyme is to vſe ye catch at his legg w^{t} ye edge of his byll, as in y^{e} ſecond ground above is ſaid.

4. Rememb^{r} euer in al yor fyght w^{t} this weapon to make yor ſpace narrow whether it be againſt the ſtaf or byll ſo y^{t} what ſo euer he ſhal do againſt you, yō ſhal ſtill make yor ward before he be in his ful force to offend you.

5. Alſo yf yō can reach w^{t}in the hed of his byll w^{t} the hed of yor byll then ſodainly w^{t} the hed of yor byll ſnach his byll hed ſtrongly towards you, & therw^{t}all indirect his byl hed & forcibly run vp yor byl hed to his hands, ſo haue yō the lyke advantage as abouеſaid, wheras I ſpake of runyng vp towards his hands.

6. Yf he lye alowe w^{t} his byl hed then yf yō can put yor byll hed in ou^{r} the hed of his bylle & ſtronglye put doune his byl ſtaf w^{t} yor byl hed, bearinge it flat, then yō may p^{r}ſently run vp yor byll hed ſingle handed to his hands & fly out therw^{t}, ſo ſhal yō hurt him in ye hand & go free yo^{r}ſelf.

7. The like may yō do w^{t} yor byll againſt the ſhort ſtaf yf yō can preſs it doune in ye lyke ſort, but yf he haue a longe ſtaf then run vp dubble handed w^{t} both hands vpon yor byll, wch thynge yō may ſafly do becauſe yō are in yor ſtrength & haue taken him in the weak prte of his ſtaf.

8. Yf he lye hye w^{t} his byll hed then put vp yor byll hed und^{r} his & caſt his byll out to y^{t} ſyde y^{t} yō ſhal fynd fytteſt, ſo haue yō the aduantage to thruſt or hook at him & fly out.

Or yf yō caſt his byl farr out of the right lyne then run in & take him by the legg w^{t} ye edge of yor byll, as is ſaid in the 2nd ground of this chapter.

Yf yō ward his blow w^{t} yor byll ſtaf w^{t}in yor byll 9.
hed, then anſwer him as w^{t} y^{e} ſhort ſtaf.

Note y^{t} as the byl mans aduantage is to tak the ſtaf w^{t} ye hed of ye byll ſo the ſtaf man by reaſon y^{t} ye hed of ye byll is a faire mark hath ye aduantage of him in ye caſting aſyde of the hed of the byll w^{t} his ſtaf or beating y^{t} aſyde, the wch yf ye byll man looke not very well into it the ſtaf man ther vpon wil take al mann^{r} of aduantages of y^{e} ſtaf fyght againſt him.

"The Chapter on the Morris pike is unique, as no other work ſpeaks of parries with that weapon."—W. London.

Of the fyght of ye morris pyke againſt the lyke weapon.

Cap: 14.

YF yō fight w^{t} yor enemy having both morris 1.
pyks w^{t} both poynts of yor pyks forwards, alowe upon ye ground, holding the butt end of the pyke in one hand ſyngle w^{t} knuckles vpwards & the thumb undrneth, w^{t} the thumbe & forefing^{r} towards yor face & the lyttle fynger towards the poynt of ye pyke, bering the butt end of the pyke frō the one ſyde to ye other right before the face, then lye yō w^{t} yor arme ſpent & yor body open w^{t} yor hand to ye right ſyde w^{t} yor knuckles Dounwards & yor nailes vpwards.

Or yō may lye in y^{t} ſort, w^{t} yor hand over to the left ſyde w^{t} yor knuckles vpwards & yor nayles Dounwards, wherby al yor body wilbe Open. yf then he ſhal ſodainlye rayſe vp the point of his pyke w^{t} his other

hand

hand & com to thruſt at yō, then in the Mountinge of his poynt or his cōynge in ſodainlye toſſe vp the poynt of yor pyke w^{t} yor hand ſyngle & ſo thruſt him in the leggs w^{t} yor pyke & fly out therw^{t}.

Or els you May ſtand vpō yor ward & Not toſſe vp yor pykes poynt but breake his thruſt by croſſynge the poynt of his pyke w^{t} the Mydds of yor pyke by caſting vp yor hand, w^{t} the butt end of yor pyke aboue yor hed, & ſo bering ouer hys point w^{t} yor ſtaf, to the other ſyde as for example,

2. Yf yō lye w^{t} yor hand ſpent towards the left ſyde of yor bodye, then ſodainlye bere his poynt ouer ſtrongly towards yor right ſyde.

Yf yō lye w^{t} yor hand ſpent towards yor right ſyde then bere his poynt towards yor left ſyde, & ther vpon gather vp yor pyke w^{t} yor other hand & thruſt at him & fly out.

Yf he cōtynew his fyght w^{t} his point aboue, & yō lye w^{t} yor pyke breſt hye & hyer w^{t} your hand & point ſo, y^{t} yō may Make yor thruſt at his face or body w^{t} yor poynt Directly towards his face, holding yor pyke w^{t} both your hands on yor ſtaf yor hinder hand w^{t} yor knuckles vpwards & yor formuſt hand w^{t} yor knuckles dounwards & ther ſhaking yor pyke & faulſing at his face w^{t} yor poynt as Neere his face as you may, then ſodainlye Make out yor thruſt ſyngle handed at his face & fly backe w^{t}all, wch thruſt he can hardly breake one of 20 by reaſon y^{t} yō haue made yor ſpace ſo narrow vpon his gard, ſo y^{t} yō beinge firſt in yor action he wil ſtil be to late in his defence to defend himſelf.

4. but note while yō lye faulſinge to Deceve him looke well to yor leggs y^{t} he in the Meane tyme toſſe not vp the

poynt of his pyke ſyngle handed & hurt yō therw^{t} in y^{e} ſhynes.

Yf he lye ſo w^{t} his poynt vp a loft as you do then 5.
Make yor ſpace Narrow Mountinge yor point a lyttle & croſe his pyke w^{t} yo^{n} & ſtronglye and ſodainly caſt his poynt out of the right lyne and thruſt whome from the ſame ſyngle or dubble as you fynd yor beſt aduantage, & fly out therw^{t}.

Or yō may run in when yō haue caſt out his poynt ſlydinge both yor hands on yor ſtaf til yō com w^{t}in iij quarters of a yard of the hed of yor pyke & ſtabb him therw^{t} w^{t} one hand & w^{t} yor other hand kepe him of from ye grype.

Now yf he be a man of ſkyll, notw^{t}ſtandinge ye 6.
Making of y^{t} faulte in ſuffering you to do ſo yet this help he hath, as yō are cōmynge in he will ſodainlye draw in his pyke poynt & fly back w^{t}all, then haue yō no helpe but to fly out inſtantly to the myddle of yor pyke & from thence backe to ye end & then are yō as at the firſt begynnynge of yor fyght yō were.

Yf you fynd y^{t} he lye farr out of ye right lyne w^{t} 7.
his poynt or y^{t} yō can ſo farr Indirect y^{e} ſame then caſt yor pyke out of yor hands, croſe over vpon the myds of his pyke, by wch meanes yō ſhal entangle his pyke, then while he doth ſtryve to get his pyke at lybertye, run you in ſodainlye drawing yor Dagg^{r} & ſtrike or ſtabb at him.

Then yf he haue the prfection of this fyght as well 8.
as you, he wilbe as reddy w^{t} his dagg^{r} as yō are w^{t} yo^{n}, then muſt yō fyght it out at the ſyngle dagg^{r} fyght as is ſhewed in the 15th Cap: then he y^{t} hath not the prfection of y^{t} fyght gow^{t} to wracke.

And

9. And here note y^t in al the course of my teachinge of these my breef Instructions yf both the prtyes haue the ful prfection of ye true fyght then the on will not be able to hurt thother at what prfyt weapon so euer.

10. But yf a Man y^t haue the prfection of fight shal fight w^t on y^t haue it not then must y^t vnskylful man go to wrack & thother goe free.

Of the single Dagger fyght against the lyke weapon. *Cap:* 15.

1. FIRST know y^t to this weapon ther belongeth no Wards nor gryps but against such a one as is foolehardy & will suffer himself to haue a ful stabb in the face or bodye to hazard the geving of Another, then against him yō may vse yor left hand in throwinge him asyde or strike vp his heeles aft^r yō haue stab^d him.

2. In this dagg^r fyght, yō must vse cōtynual motion so shal he not be able to put yō to ye cloze or grype, because yor contynuall motion disappointeth him of his true place, & the more ferce he is in runynge in, the soon^r he gayneth you the place, wherby he is wounded, & yō not any thing the rather endangered.

3. The mann^r of handling yor cōtynuall motion is this, kepe out of distance & strik or thrust at his hand, Arme, face or body, y^t shal press vpon yō, & yf he defend blow or thrust w^t his dagg^r make yō blow or thrust at his hand.

4. Yf he com in w^t his left legg forewards or w^t the right, do you strike at y^t prte as soone as it shalbe w^tin yor reach, remembring y^t yō vse contynual motion in

in yor prgreſſion & regreſſyon according to yor twyfold gou^{r}nors.

Although the dagg^{r} fyght be thought a verye dan- 5.
gerous fyght by reaſon of y^{e} ſhortnes & ſynglenes
therof, yet the fight therof being handled as is aforeſaid, is as ſaf & as defencive as is the fight of any other
weapon, this endeth my breef Inſtructions.

Finis.

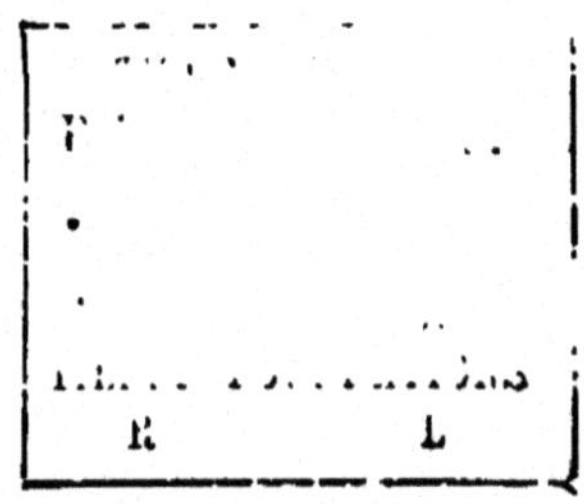
R
L

Open fight

open fight is to carry yor [illegible] & hilt aloft above yor head either wth ye point

- 1 upright
- 2 backwards wch is best
  - 1 best it falls best to ye gardant ward
  - 2 yt these wch you find aloft to
    - strike
    - thrust
    - ward,

Of ye best single sword against ye like weapon being both of on length,

1 answere him in ye same fight is best. but keepe your distance

2 let yor gatherings be ever towards his right side yt yor sword may crosse all his blowes made at yow, wch must be in force & from yor ward instantly move & strike him on ye head or other open place, or thrust him in ye body & instantly fly out

1 if yor enemy [illegible] in open or true gardant fight

- 3 if he strike at ye
  - 1 left
    - side of [illegible] head or body
      - 1 ward it wth ye [illegible] true gardant ward
        - take it wth ye true gardant ward, [illegible]
        - yt yow do wch at [illegible] strike
        - wch al-[illegible] from yor ward [illegible] thrust
        - & strike from ye ward [illegible]
        - at ye head, arm or thrust at ye body
          - 1 press in to close [illegible] ye grips of him
          - 2 if he [illegible] al[illegible] go not in, then instantly crosse & strike him on ye head & fly out,
  - 2 right
    - 2 then put downe yor hilt aloft &
      - 1 mount yor point, so yt yor blade be cast out on his left towards yor right shoulder & so will ye ward ye right side of yor head from wch [illegible] strike instantly at his left side of [illegible] head body thigh
      - 2 [illegible] his right [illegible] & fly back [illegible] on [illegible] [illegible] aloft
  - 3 [illegible] in [illegible] fight, [illegible] at his hand or arme by [illegible] yor point wth yor knuckles downwards & fly out instantly

2 if he thrust at yor face or body, then beat it downwards wth yor [illegible] gardant, carrying yor point [illegible] [illegible] yor right side & [illegible] strike him on ye head or thrust him in ye body & fly out [illegible]

Facsimile Table of "Open Fight" in the MS. of "Bref Instructions."

(Readjusted on folding table following page 134.)

4 forwardly press on yo wth ye fight intendinge to hurt yo in ye face or eyes / or to take ye grype of yo /

Against him yt useth both open & gardant fight, yo shal[l] upon every blow or thrust made at yo, shifte yor weapon & strike or thrust him, on ye face hed or body, & fly out instantly /

yf he in his open or true gardant fight 2 & yo lye below in variable fight, then other not to [illegible] 2 ye blowe made at yor hed in true gardant ward —

1 But at forehand ward, & be sure to kepe yor distance: to make him come in wth his feet or feet & yt will disappoint his tyme & place

2 { 1 thrust wilbe to longe / 2 space to to wide } in due tyme to do it,

3 answer him not in ye bastard / imperfect gardant fight, wth yor body comming forwards either yo:

1 ye space wilbe to wide on both sydes to make a true ward in due tyme

2 arme & body wilbe open to more harme, so yt as bending in of ye body in ye tyme of ye hand or hand & feet he may either thrust yor body or take ye grype of yo /

yf he fight upon open fight

2 { first, first breaking his distance, & do attempt to strike at ye open hed, strike surely [illegible] on ye hed him [illegible] [illegible] at in his coming in, and [illegible] for yt maketh an [illegible] slip a little back [illegible], for yt maketh a true [illegible] yor blow [illegible] his hed & maketh a true ward for yor owne

2 it is better for ye patient to strike home strongly at ye agents hed, if ye agent press upon him to win ye place, then to thrust. For ye reason last aforesaid / [illegible] gardant fight, mind ward true for [illegible]

yo fight upon open or true gardant fight [illegible] to wide in due tyme to make a true ward, for ye space wilbe to wide in due tyme [illegible] ye manner of ye imbrocata [illegible] a loft at his point [illegible] ye, after ye manner of ye [illegible] upwards then put him make yor space narrow wth ye point [illegible] & strike or thrust as aforesaid at any open place by his point & strike or thrust & fly out presently but be sure ever to kepe yor distance

2 { & he deceive yo not in ye taking his point /

Sundry kinds of play or fight.   *Thornborow.*

1 Unc^{r}taine variable
2 ſyngle
3 gardant.

iij different kinds of fight.

1 y^{t} forceth or p^{r}ſſeth on
2 he y^{t} goeth back w^{t} ſom blow or thruſt
3 he y^{t} ſtandeth to his wards or paſſato

} w^{t} an Imp^{r}fit ward & out of ye way.

1. Againſt him y^{t} p^{r}ſſeth y^{e}, naked play is beſt becs he uſeth his foote, ye open lofty play ye hand.

2. ye 2nd is beſt followed w^{t} ye variable & vnc^{r}taine handling els ſhould yō be a ma^{r}ke to yor enemy & too ſlow in motion.

3. ye 3rd muſt be incountred w^{t} ye gardant play wherin you ſhal try him at ye B ſword or how he can eſcape ye prting blow or thruſt.

When yō gather kepe yor place & ſpace equal & only be a patient & rememb^{r} y^{t} ye gardant play bringeth yō ſafly in & keps yor enemy out.

Know this ord^{r} of play els ye beſt may be deceaved, to be uſed againſt al theſe differencs & bring ye goodnes therof in ſuſpitiō, for al theſe plaies are good in their kynd, tyme & occaſiō offered by div^{r}ſitie of play, but not on of them to be continually uſed & played vpon as a p^{r}fectiō againſt euery aſſault.

1. In ye naked play yō muſt ſet yo^{r}ſelf vpright w^{t} yor feet in a ſmale ſpace, obſ^{r}ving ye place of yor hand wher yō may ſtrike or thruſt moſt quickly & redely & ſo take ye tyme of him y^{t} p^{r}ſſeth on (vſing ye tyme of his feet) w^{t} yor blowe or thruſt wher he is moſt open.

1. In ye variable play, yō dryve him to his ſhyfts changing yo^{r}ſelf into ſundry kynds of blowes thruſts & lyings, wch yō muſt not ſtay upon,

2. ſeeking to + him ſtil in his playes as yō may, wherby yō ſhal force him to fly, or els to ſtand to ye proof of his B ſword play.

3. the gardant play is to be vſed againſt ye blowe, thruſt & paſſata y^{t} cometh w^{t}in dang^{r} of hurt, for treading ye right way & keping yor place & hand in ſpace & ſtrength you cannot looſe ye tyme to defend frō either of thoſe offers.

theſe Judged of in reaſon & known by ſom practiſe wil make yō deale ſafly againſt al ſorts, ſkilful or vnſkilful, ſo y^{t} feare or Ang^{r} hinder not yor Knowledge.

Of Tymes.

1. The tyme of y^{e} { hand
   foote
   hand & foot
   foot & hand. naught

Of

Of place ſpace. ſtrength & tyme.

1. ye tyme of ye hand is when yō ſtrike frō a w^{rd} or ſtand in place to ſtrike.

2. the tyme of ye foot is when yō ſtep forward to ſtrike or when yō gather towarde yor own right ſyde.

3. ye tyme of ye hand & foot is when yō tread yor ground in courſe to ſtrike rather than p^rſſing forwards, or when yō ſlide back or go back, yor hand & foot being then of equal agillitie.

4. y^e tyme of y^e foot & hand is when yō handle yor gardant play vſing then a ſlowe motiō in both.

ther is but i good way to gather vpō yor enemy, gardant. Al other are dangerous & ſubiect to y^e blowe on y^e hed or thruſt on y^e body.

for no way can ward both but as $aforſ^d$.

yor hand & feet in good play muſt go together, whether it be in quick or ſlow motion.

In gathering forwards or $tow^{rd}s$ yor right ſyde yor hand falleth frō yor place, ſpace, & ſtrength & ſo falleth out y^e loſs of tyme.

when yō gather & ſuffer y^t gou^rne yor fight, defend only. when yō do, be ſingle, or not fixed towards on any lying, but alſo y^e quicknes of yor hand in its p^rp^r place carried,

In breaking ye thruſt when yō lye aloft ſingle or gardant & ſpace yor arme ſomwhat bowing in warding y^e blowe, haue reſpect to yor place of hand & ſtrength, yor arme ſtrait. this courſe in yor tyme is beſt p^rformed, the on of theſe w^t yor hand aloft yor point downe thother yor hand in place yor more high yor ſpace leſs curious.

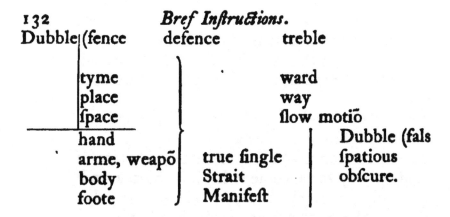

Dubble (fence defence treble

tyme		ward	
place		way	
ſpace		ſlow motiō	
hand			Dubble (fals
arme, weapō	true ſingle		ſpatious
body	Strait		obſcure.
foote	Manifeſt		

II tyme is cheefly to be obſrved in both actions vpō

93re wch (place / ſpace) waiteth.

Upon theſe 3 ye 4 following, vpon theſe 4 ye firſt 3, upon theſe ye later 3.

to hurt or defend, a tyme in both is to be obſrved to ye furtherance of wch place is to be gotten, wtout wch tyme wilbe to long to prform yt wch is intended, ye ſpace is to be noted betwene ij oppoſits & in reſpect of touching, or in regard of ſaving as alſo for prſving of tyme, by ye ſmale way it hath either to ye body, or puting by ye weapon.

the next 4 muſt be vſed together to prforme thother iij rules, for ye hand being nymble & quick of itſelf may els be hindered in ye want of any of theſe, the weapon muſt be framed & inclyned to ſrve ye agilitie of ye hand eyther in hurting or defending.

4 □ the body vpright or leanyng to ye weapon, yt it hindr not ye diſpoſitiō of thother ij the foot anſwerable to them plying ye hand & ward al in ſtrait ſpace, ye wrd wt hand high wt ye point downe, the arme ſtrait out as redy for both actions.

the

the way vndr ye wrd wtdrawing ye body from harmes, the motiō ſlowe yt ye actiō of ye hand be not hindered.

the reſt are ye diſpoſitions of ye placed diſplaced handlings

Slowfoot : ſwift hand : quick foot : ſlow hand.

tread : ſtride : follow : falaway :

When yō ſeek to offend wt blow or thruſt, yor place of hand is loſt, ye way to redeeme it is to ſlyde back vndr yor lofty ward as aforeſd alwaies yt yor adurſarie lye aloft redy to ſtrike or thruſt or vſe his hand only,

yf yō would offend him yt lyeth lowe vpō ye thruſt then when yō diſplace yor weapon frō aloft yō may aftr yor blow at hed or arme or neereſt place, ſtand & thruſt before yō go backe becauſe he is out of place & ſpace & cannot +, & therby looſeth his tyme to annoy yō & yō may thruſt & retyre for a new aſſault.

this not ſo ſownd,

In ſtriking or thruſting neur hindr yor hand wt puting forth yor foote but kepe ye place therof til yō haue offended wt ye one only ye bending of yor body very little foreward may ſufficte, els yō looſe a dubble tyme, on in ſetting forth yor foot thother in recouring yor loſt place of yor fōt both to ye loſs of tyme & yor purpoſte.

Strike : thruſt : ward : breake :

the dubble offence is in ſtriking & thruſting.

the iij fold defence in { warding ye blow
breaking or puting bye ye thruſt
ſlyding back vndr yor hanging ward.

wyn ye place : ſtand faſt, ſtrike home
offend, defend, & go ſaf.

al vndr play is beaten wt moſt agil, ſingle & ye lofty the lofty wt ye gardant, His when wt his foot he

ſeeke ye low lying is out of place to ofend defend or not ſo for lack of tyme ſpace & croſſing, yf he lye out wt his longr weapō it is put bye frō aloft, who hath place tyme & reach of body & arme al wt ye +.	93 re ye reading ye enterlyyinge of other things therto adioyning.

the lofty naked play is beaten wt ye ward becs of	Croſs ſpace tyme

to Defend, ye lofty naked ſingle looſe play ſrveth to win ye Tyme of ye lowe & dubble play.

the bent gardant requireth yor arme ſtrait high & out ye point down towards (93 re II wel) ye body & foote yt way inclyned.

CHISWICK PRESS:—CHARLES WHITTINGHAM AND CO.
TOOKS COURT, CHANCERY LANE, LONDON.

Lightning Source UK Ltd.
Milton Keynes UK
UKOW07f2204300717
306334UK00015B/455/P

9 781293 966839